# Breaking Barriers

## Decisions that Elevate People From Ordinary to Extraordinary

### An Anthology by Enlightened Authors

### Compiled by Best-Selling Author
# JIM T. CHONG

# BREAKING BARRIERS

## Compiled by Best-Selling Author
## Jim T. Chong

These works are based on actual events. In certain cases, incidents, characters, and timelines have been changed for dramatic purposes to protect the privacy of the individuals.

## Let someone else's unbelief be the fuel for you to do the Extraordinary!

"There are only two paths in life: a screwed up one or a righteousness one. I chose the righteousness path. I did it by ignoring limits and not listening to others tell me all the BS about why I couldn't achieve my goals. Nevertheless, I believe that the impossible is possible.

Just remember...if you never risk going too far, you will never know how far you can go. By reading this book, it will help you overcome your fears and barriers that will give you the confidence you need to succeed."

### ~ Kirby Delaunay

World Record Brick Breaking Champion

Record holder for breaking the most bricks in 2016: 150 bricks in 1 minute and 33 seconds, soon to beat her own record with 300 bricks to break.

On the set of the most diverse and best show on MONEY 1055FM …Rush Hour for Success!

Pictured: Frank Casanova (SacFilmZine.online), Richard Dixon (SAG Actor), Jim Meyer (Realtor / Producer of Jackson Bolt & Soul Cage), Jane Taff "The Sage"), Kirby Delaunay World Record Holder), Mel Martin (FitLuvStrong), Jim T. Chong "The Wok Star", and Michael Delaunay.

Because sometimes we need that example,
that one degree,
that story of inspiration to help us believe.

"I PRESENT TO YOU…
the EXTRAORDINARY AUTHORS of:

***BREAKING BARRIERS -
Decisions That Elevate People
From Ordinary to Extraordinary.***"

**Jim T. Chong, Compiler**

# TABLE OF CONTENTS

# ACKNOWLEDGEMENTS

I want to first off thank God, Mom (who has passed on), Dad, my sister Patty, and my kids. A special thanks to my Life Coach Jane Taff, Mary Nicholson, and to my mentors Eric Antonio, Chet Finley, Kathy Fairbanks, Jim Stovall, and Roger Palmieri. Also, I am indebted to those that have believed in me and supported me in my lifetime in very specific ways, such as John and Thien Pask, Chris Lambert, and Mai Nguyen. There are many others that have been so instrumental in helping me become who I am today.

I personally thank each author who has put up with the rolling dates to make this book happen as I took care of some important life situations. I must also share my extreme gratitude to my co-publisher, Nichole Peters, who has been my rock and example in this process.

There are many others that have been so instrumental in helping me become who I am today.

*Jim T. Chong*

ঔ ◆ ৵

On the behalf of Believe In Your Dreams Publishing, we would like to express an abundance of gratitude, love, and blessings to Jim T. Chong. Thank you for trusting the Believe In Your Dreams Publishing and Production team with your amazing project. May your great book BREAK BARRIERS across the globe.

Believe In Your Dreams Publishing would like to extend further appreciation to every co-author who shared their heartfelt true stories to the masses. I pray each story will touch and heal the lives of many people across this great nation. Thanks for believing in me and my rocking team. We love, adore, and appreciate you all.

**CEO, Nichole Peters**
**Believe In Your Dreams Publishing**

# PREFACE
## "What's the Difference Between Being Ready FOR Change and Being Ready TO Change?"
### By Roger Palmieri

> It's not that some people have willpower and some don't. It's that some people are ready to change and others are not.
>
> TIME For CHANGE

I BELIEVE STRUGGLE AND LIFE circumstances are given to each of us to show us what we are really made of inside. Each obstacle is an opportunity to discover the depth of who we are and who we consciously choose to be. My life path has shown me, without a doubt, that we each have the ability to make our life into what we want it to be. In fact, it became my life mission to learn to do this for myself. Then it became my passion to share what I have learned and to be a guide and an example to others who want to make significant lasting changes in their lives. This passion drives my life.

Of course, I did not know these things until later in my life. First, I had to learn to rise above obstacles. I had to reach a low point in my emotional struggles before I was open to receiving the gift of divine intervention. I had to search, study, experiment, and go through good ole' trial and error.

My obstacles began very early in my life. My parents divorced when I was only two years old and I became the rope in their emotional tug of war. I felt that I was not wanted or loved and that I did not belong. Luckily, my grandmother, aunt, and uncle showed me love and gave me some sense of belonging. Yet I began seeking another group where I felt at home. When I was twelve, a neighbor of mine introduced me to a group of surfers, and I experienced true belonging for the first time. I was tan and happy until I graduated from high school.

I "came of age" during the height of the Vietnam War. Feeling a patriotic obligation to serve my country, I enlisted in the Marine Corps, where I would meet my best friend Dave. We were deployed to Vietnam. Twenty-three days later, he was killed right in front of my eyes in a fire fight. I was overwhelmed with grief, sadness, and anger and became a changed man as I lived through the horrors of war.

When I returned to the U.S., I had no direction or purpose and was plagued with depression and all-encompassing rage. More than ever I needed family. However, nothing had changed. I tried self-medicating to ease the emotional pain. Nothing worked. Then one Thursday afternoon, I took my hopelessness, anger, pain, and disillusionment to a pew in a quiet church. I got on my knees and prayed. After a while, a feeling of peacefulness came over me. I lifted myself from my knees and sat in the pew. I noticed a crumpled piece of paper next to me, picked it up, and opened it. Scribbled on it were these words: "If it's meant to be, it's up to me."

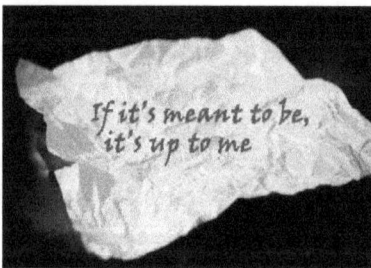

That moment changed my life. I decided then and there to do whatever it takes to live a purposeful life and to make a positive difference.

My first project was myself. I wanted to change and improve my attitudes and habits. I began talking to others about my newfound direction and realized I was not alone. Many people wanted to create lasting, positive change in their lives, but didn't know how. I became hungry to find out how people, including me, could improve their lives.

I enrolled in college and began taking evening psychology classes while I worked during the day. Always an avid reader (I began reading the Encyclopedia Britannica at age seven), I studied psychology, philosophy, how our minds work, and the writings of great teachers throughout history such as Aristotle, Plato, Socrates, Jesus, Buddha, and current teachers such as Earl Nightingale, Napoleon Hill, Og Mandino, Zig Ziglar, Jim Rohn, Bob Proctor, Buckminister Fuller, Doug Edwards, Cavett Robert, Werner Erhard, B.F. Skinner, and many, many others.

As I studied and practiced what I was learning, I started creating my life by design rather than by chance. People began to notice. They wanted to know what I was doing, and I shared my ideas and experiences. They suggested I share this information with as many people as I could. That was over thirty-eight years ago. I stood up, looked myself in the eyes, felt my heart beating, and dared to step up and create a life worth living.

My dreams began to come true. They still are. Over the years, my BIG DREAM has gotten bigger and bigger. I am still learning, growing, and sharing. I stay focused on being the best I can be and serving others to the best of my ability. And my Big Dreams keep coming true. Every day, for this, I am extremely grateful.

## THE PSYCHOLOGY OF CHANGE

One of the most asked questions I receive from people in my Performance Workshops centers around the Psychology of Change.

People facing any kind of change often experience similar emotions and have to go through a similar process.

I liken the process that happens to that experience of when someone close to you passes away. There are defined stages that people experience, and depending what stage you're in, you'll be making big changes in your behaviors that will bring a change in your life.

**Lots of people are ready for things to change around them. (Ain't that the truth?) Pay attention to people around you for the next five days and I'll bet you'll hear people say things like:**

"If I could only have more (money, time, energy, etc.), things would be different."

"When I win the lottery, I will do something extraordinary."

"If I only had more prospects in my pipeline..."

"Stuff keeps getting in my way."

"Why aren't things getting better for me? It's not fair!"

These people feel they are ready for change to happen to them. However, they lack the "Mind-Set" that allows them to **DO SOMETHING** about their own situation. Instead, they stay in a place of circumstance, blame, and helplessness. The first step in the psychology of changing one's behavior is to **Increase the Urgency!**

Until you feel that changing is urgent, you aren't going to change. You might think about change and wish for it, even pray for it, but until you are pulled out of your comfort zone and the urgency is clear to you, lasting change won't happens.

Think about the last successful event (closed sale, diet, exercise) you went on. What were the motivating factors to make you wake up one day and decide, "Today is the day!"? I would wager it was a sense of urgency that something must be done. Something happened to make your urgency increase, and this made you take the small steps towards change that day that you needed to take. It's the same in pretty much every area of our lives.

Until you're ready <u>TO</u> change, and not just ready FOR change, you probably won't make any progress towards your goals. If you're stuck and can't figure out why, this might be it! You might not be ready yet and you need to push through the other stages of change that are necessary for your urgency to increase. This is true in every aspect of our lives.

Another way of looking at this is the Change Curve below. Change is a process, and it isn't really until you get to step 4 that things really start to change! The first four steps feel pretty rotten, but they can also go really fast if you don't let yourself get stuck in them.

You can see that the curve goes down before it goes up. This shows how you probably feel about life during these early stages. Once you do get through the letting go phase, things start feeling fantastic! **And when you stick with it, your <u>Motivation</u> and <u>Productivity</u> actually goes higher than they were before you made the change.**

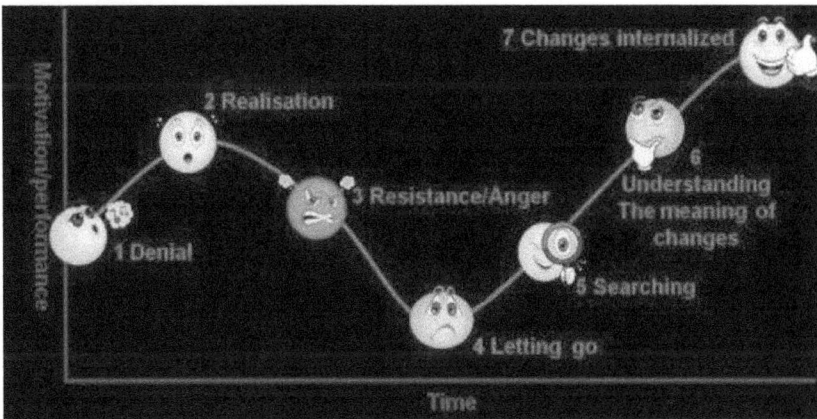

So where are you on this curve?

Are you still just waiting for your life to change around you, or are you ready <u>TO</u> make your life change?

If it's the latter, it's time to get yourself into one of my Workshops, or else 2018 will be a repeat of 2017, and you are better than that!

If not, it's time to look a bit deeper into those excuses you're telling yourself.

**Change starts with this one moment,
with one choice,
and with one small action.**

*"May all of your dreams become reality
and all of your efforts
become magnificent achievements"*

**~Roger~**

**~ For more information ~
Contact Roger at**

<u>DREAMBIG@ThePalmieriGroup.com</u>

**and visit my website –
ThePalmieriGroup.com**

**#1 Bestselling Author ...
The Prosperity Factor . . .**

**Dream Big ... I <u>DARE</u> YOU**

# FOREWORD
## By Jim Stovall

Dear Reader:

I want to compliment you for investing your time and money into this book. As my late, great friend, mentor, and publisher Charlie "Tremendous" Jones said, "You will be the same person you are today five years from now except for the people you meet and the books you read." Within these pages, you are going to read an exceptional book and meet some exceptional people.

I first met Jim Chong through my work with Klemmer and Associates and my Millionaire Institute event. Jim is a leader in the best sense of that word and someone worthy of being followed, both personally and professionally.

I'm a big believer in the fact that you should never take advice from anyone who doesn't have what you want. You are fortunate as, within this book, you are going to meet a number of people who represent different backgrounds, professions, and lifestyles who collectively can offer virtually anyone the key to anything they want.

I have written over thirty books to date, and seven of them have been turned into movies with several more in production. I have long believed that if you can tell a great story, you earn the right to share your message. The co-authors of *Breaking Barriers: Decisions that Elevate People from Ordinary to Extraordinary* all have great stories to tell and powerful messages to share.

Among other treasures in this book, you will learn that you have the right to choose, and those choices will impact every area of your life going forward; we impact everyone we meet and are impacted by them; our life's choices are serious because this is not a practice game; and we can learn from both obstacles and epiphanies. I know you will enjoy these stories and be inspired by them, but my greatest hope is that you will internalize these messages and change your life and the lives of everyone with whom you come in contact.

I am looking forward to your success!

Jim Stovall
2018

## *MEET JIM STOVALL...*

In spite of blindness, Jim Stovall has been a National Olympic weightlifting champion, a successful investment broker, the President of the Emmy Award-winning Narrative Television Network, and a highly sought-after author and platform speaker. He is the author of 30 books, including the bestseller, *The Ultimate Gift*, which is now a major motion picture from 20th Century Fox starring James Garner and Abigail Breslin. Five of his other novels have also been made into movies with two more in production.

Steve Forbes, president and CEO of Forbes magazine, says, "Jim Stovall is one of the most extraordinary men of our era."

For his work in making television accessible to our nation's thirteen million blind and visually impaired people, The President's Committee on Equal Opportunity selected Jim Stovall as the Entrepreneur of the Year. Jim Stovall has been featured in *The Wall Street Journal, Forbes magazine, USA Today*, and has been seen on *Good Morning America, CNN, and CBS Evening News*. He was also chosen as the International Humanitarian of the Year, joining Jimmy Carter, Nancy Reagan, and recently canonized Saint Teresa of Calcutta as recipients of this honor.

# THE NIGHT MY WORLD CHANGED
*By Tim Beglin*

Was it a premonition, or perhaps some sort of sixth sense?

At the time, with final exams starting the following week, I chalked it up to a nervous night's sleep. Like most students, I had gone home for the long Memorial Day holiday weekend and had just gotten back to my dorm earlier that evening. It was my first year away at college, around three o'clock in the morning when I suddenly found myself out of bed, pacing the hallways of my dorm for no apparent reason.

Although it was many years ago, I remember being incredibly lucid as I walked the hallways, despite the early morning hour. To this day, I still recall consciously thinking, "What the hell am I even doing awake?" After a few laps up and down the deserted hallway, in spite of never concluding why I was awake in the first place, I eventually managed to get back to sleep for what was left of the night.

Less than six short hours later and class well underway, the door of my economics classroom opened and the dean of the business school walked in. I immediately sensed the news was for me, and I knew it was not going to be good. In fact, by the time the dean and professor simultaneously turned to look at me, I had already packed up my things and was making my way to the front of the classroom.

I remember walking down the long hallway toward the exit of the business school building with the dean beside me, on our way to his office. There were a couple of eerie things about that walk. One, it was just the two of us in this usually very busy and noisy corridor. Two, for some unknown reason, as we walked down the hallway I felt as if I was alone, walking down a very long tunnel.

Although the center of my vision was clear, everything on the periphery was foggy and spinning like a kaleidoscope.

My dad was only in his forties. There were no earlier signs that he would have a massive heart attack. He was pronounced dead earlier that morning, at about three o'clock. He left behind seven children and a woman who still loves him to this day. We were such a young family, and losing him left us all feeling alone and scared. It felt so final, and yet somehow we had to learn to go on, knowing that what was left behind would never be the same again.

With such a large family, we certainly didn't have too much of anything, but our parents worked hard to make sure we were fine. I remember that every so often, Mom and Dad would take us out for Dollar Mondays at a local restaurant, where each plate was really only $1! Those nights were so much fun for us. As you can imagine, we didn't get to go out as a family very often, so when we did, it was pretty special.

I was the only one in our family who wasn't home that awful night. I have wondered many, many times, both when he died and since that day, whether there was any meaning to me not being there when it happened. The only conclusion I have ever come to was that, meaning or not, our dad was gone.

Once I returned to school after the funeral services, I vividly remember sitting alone in my dorm room and consciously saying to myself, "Okay, now what? This is not the way life is supposed to happen. What do we do now? What do I do now? I can't believe he is gone! This has shattered and changed everything. Home can never really be home again." And then I began to cry.

Many families have hard times to overcome. For any of us seven kids to go to college was a pretty big deal. But now, with the loss of my dad, there was an ominous financial weight crashing down on me - and on any of my siblings who wanted to continue their education after high school too. Dad had been our safety net, our everything. Knowing Mom had enough to do just trying to piece life back together for herself and everyone else left at home, I didn't feel I could burden her any further with my issues. At that moment, I felt so alone and vulnerable, living hundreds of miles away from a home I emotionally could never go back to.

Another part of my new normal was the realization that I would not be able to stay in college unless I performed well academically and paid for it myself. Beyond facing that term's finals, I had to figure out how I was going to pay for the rest of my college education - because I told myself that quitting school was not an option. Somehow, while still in a lingering fog from my dad's death, I managed to pass my finals and cobble together enough university hardship loans to make it through the year.

Over my first summer break, I worked sixty hour weeks at the same fast food restaurant where I had worked all through high school. I wanted to make as much money as I could to supplement the gaps in my financial aid. When we all went back to school after the summer, I was taken aback that my roommate, Freddie, didn't return. He was on a full-ride football scholarship. The only thing he had to do to maintain his scholarship was learn the new playbook over the summer, and he didn't even do that. So he lost his entire scholarship, and out of school he went. Here he'd been given a physical gift, and he'd wasted it.

Juan was my new roommate. The only thing we had in common was that neither of us had any money, but we really got along well and were very supportive of one another. The mysterious thing about Juan was that every so often, he would leave school for two or three days. He wouldn't say he was leaving, he would just be gone. Then he would just show back up again a few days later. The story around the dorm was that he was bringing Mexicans over the border to the United States. I asked him about it once, and he just smiled and said he was helping his uncle out. That was the only time we ever spoke a single word about it. After graduating, we lost touch. I heard that Juan went on to become a very successful psychiatrist, but unfortunately, he died from cancer when he was only in his forties.

After four and a half years in college (I changed majors early on, so it took me another half year), I graduated from the university magna cum laude with a degree in accounting. Since I had to pay back all of my accumulated college debt, the very high employment rate for graduating accounting students was a significant factor in me changing to this major.

Here is an inside secret: I was not a gifted student, I just studied really, really hard to earn good grades. In fact, I never really enjoyed any level of school. However, after my first year away at college, I began to realize that I had a growing inner strength and a will to move forward, which I directly attributed to my dad's passing. For example, every night (and I mean every night) after dinner in the school cafeteria, my dorm mates would head back to the dorm, whereas I would head off to study alone. The library had limited hours, which was not effective for my study style, so I would go out in search of privacy.

Once I got the lay of the campus, I actually found a remote utility room in a rarely used classroom building. The night I first discovered this room, the door to the building was locked, but a window was cracked just enough for me to crawl in. I made this room my own secret study hall for the rest of my time at the university by leaving that same window unlocked every night when I left - which was long after the library had closed. I spent hours and hours studying in that room, through nights, weekends, and holidays, and I was never found out! In fact, I studied so much that on my advanced accounting final, one of the last exams I ever took at school, I scored a perfect 100%. Finding that utility room, combined with my tenacity to stay on a topic, turned out to be my secret weapon for getting through college after losing my dad. These raw but developing traits would serve me well then and I still continually find myself relying on these core attributes.

Based on my grades and the fact that I had worked my way through college, I got multiple offers from CPA firms upon graduation. I accepted an offer, borrowed some money to buy my first suit, and started my business career. As awkward and strange as it felt to be out of college and working in the "real world" for the first time, I felt surprisingly comfortable with what I was doing and the direction I was heading. Over my seven-year tenure in the public accounting profession, I got my CPA license, earned a master's degree in taxation, got married, had two boys, and was ready for another challenge. You see, although I liked public accounting and it was a really good means to an end, I always told myself that I didn't like it enough to die as a public accountant.

My first position after leaving public accounting was as vice president of an international import company. Initially, the business had its own set of challenges, but the company ended up becoming enormously successful and ultimately sold to the Hallmark Company. After coming off this very exhilarating and high profile sale, I thought my business life would soar and I would see multiple opportunities dropped at my doorstep. Yet, much like in life, everything in business does not necessarily work out the way you dreamed it would.

My next position was with a publishing company 3,000 miles away from where I lived at the time. I needed a job and beggars can't be choosers. Yet as a family, we were really unsure whether or not we would like the area enough to relocate across the country. So I started my employment there by commuting, leaving on Sundays and returning late Thursday evenings. I would travel through Chicago O'Hare Airport, back and forth and back and forth.

I was hired on to expand their national sales and operations efforts, but shortly after getting started, Ernie, the company's CEO, came to me and told me that their main supplier (a Fortune 500 company) was threating to push us into bankruptcy for lack of payment. Since I had not been privy to the finances earlier, I was completely stunned by his admission. Deeper than that, I was personally and professionally scared of what all this meant.

In spite of the world seemingly crashing down around us, Ernie and I closed our office doors, turned the phones off, and over the course of the next three days, we worked together to devise a strategy to deal with this imminent creditor threat. This plan, among other things, completely reorganized the company: I would become the new CEO and Ernie would be reassigned as head of marketing. Interestingly, the more we worked on the project, the more the initial shock of our fate began to wear off. I found the work effort following the bad news to be the best cure for those earlier personal and professional fears. Ernie and I presented the reorganization plan to that creditor's Board, and somehow, they accepted our entire reorganization proposal and agreed to give us time to work out a new debt repayment structure with them. Ernie and I were not only thrilled; we were proud and so very relieved. Of course, the two of us went out that night to celebrate!

After a great night's sleep and an even better conversation with my wife the next morning about life and priorities, I went into Ernie's office first thing that day and resigned. My six months of commuting and one day as CEO of the publishing company were over. You see, what I told Ernie was that my son had a Little League game and I needed to be there to see it. The decision was just that simple. For one of the first times in my life, I chose family over work. After talking to my wife, I knew I needed to go home for good.

Internally for the company, my leaving ended up not being that traumatic. Ernie was the leader before me and he continued as leader when I left. That day, after saying goodbye to him and the others, however, everything was a blur. The next thing I recall is sitting in O'Hare, waiting for the last commuter flight home, and thinking to myself, *I am probably the only person in this entire Frequent Flyer Club who is unemployed.* Talk about a gut check! For the first time in my young adult life, I not only didn't have a job, I'd just given away a pretty good one!

And yet, by the time my plane landed back in my hometown, I had mapped out a whole new professional life for myself. I don't know where the creative juices came from, but during that flight, I outlined a business plan and Beglin & Associates business consultants was born. I realized that day that I was pretty good at business finance and operations, but more than that, I was really, really good when others were giving up. So for the next couple of years, I would start my day in my home office scanning the local business paper, looking for companies that seemed to be teetering on bankruptcy, and I would go see them. I built up a very nice consulting practice, was able to coach both of my sons all the way through their Little League days, and from my reputation in the community, I ended up getting an employment offer I just couldn't refuse: a senior executive position at a local company.

Since that time, I have held various C-level positions for a variety of companies in a number of different industries. Each one of these companies has had its own set of issues, but at the same time, each has had its own set of rewards as well. Looking back on them, one common denominator was that each became so successful that it drew the attention of a buyer and ended up being acquired by another company. When that would happen, I would pick up my transaction bonus check and off I would go to do it again with the next company, and then again, and then again, and again.

Using the same creative juices I had on the plane ride back from Chicago, I thought about all the business do's and don'ts I've learned over the years and I wrote *Ring$ of Value: Run Your Business Every Day Like It's For Sale.* The book helps everyday owners understand how businesses are valued in a sale, but more importantly, it shows them how they can exponentially drive the value of their company beyond their wildest expectations. Armed with that level of knowledge, instead of the business running them, owners can very successfully run their business.

Business, like life itself, is what you make of it. I wasn't born with a silver spoon in my mouth, and I really didn't grow up with anyone who was. My business life didn't follow a straight line - in fact, sometimes there were gaps, holes, and pitfalls in my trek - but I don't know of anyone who has experienced the perfect career path. I also didn't have a premonition that lonely night my dad died, nor did I have any mystical insight into any of the businesses that I have helped prosper. Stuff just happens; but it's what each of us do with that stuff that makes all the difference.

My dad's death was one of the most painful experiences in my life. As time has ticked by, not only has the pain from that night stayed with me, I also feel new sorrow because my dad has now missed out on more life than he got to live. He never met my wife or got to hear the little ones in his life go from calling him Dad to Grandpa and now even Great-grandpa. Many, many times I have imagined myself calling him for advice, or just to hear his voice. What hurts the most is what we didn't get to do and see together.

Yet what I found out about myself the night my world changed is that a level of inner strength and clarity resides in me and, frankly, in all of us. It is a gear that can kick in at our most desperate times-we just have to realize it is there and carefully use it. To this day, when things around me, in my business or my personal life, are in complete mayhem, I wait for the fog in my head to lift, the kaleidoscope in the background to settle, and my tunnel vision to focus. That is my inner strength showing up again to help me through the moment, and for that, I thank you, Dad.

Now, go find your inner strength and do something you never dreamed you could do before!

## MEET TIM BEGLIN...

Tim Beglin is the author of ***Ring$ of Value: Run Your Business Everyday Like It's For Sale***. This book about business valuations does two things:

• First, it helps owners and entrepreneurs understand how to calculate the value of their own company and,

• Second, it shows these high achievers what they can do to actually drive exponential value their own enterprise.

The book is available on-line through both Amazon and Barnes & Noble.

Tim has held various C-level positions with companies in different industries and also has invested in other ventures. Through these experiences, he has been involved with many successful business transactions from both the buyer and seller perspectives. More important, he has spearheaded the process for other companies, leading up to their successful transactions.

As a principal with Target Advisory Services, Tim has incorporated these experiences into the consulting practice to bring this deep knowledge to businesses large and small as they go through the roller coaster of running their business or prepare for their own transaction.

Tim is a CPA, holds a master's degree in taxation, and is a guest corporate speaker.

For more information about Tim Beglin or the variety of services offered by Target Advisory Services, please visit the company's website at www.targetadvisoryservices.com.

# WHEN LIFE TRIES TO TAKE YOU DOWN
*By Jim T. Chong*

*"As you face various challenges and barriers in life,
they are opportunities for growth and indicators
of just how badly you want something."*

When we are younger, the world is our stage. We feel almost invincible and able to accomplish almost anything in life. However, as we encounter situations that challenge us, they make us pause and attempt to condition us to avoid risk and adversity. It is almost like a dance where we seek to move forward to achieve something significant in life, but life itself makes us step back and warns us how important it is to play safe causing as we go forward to retreat and go backwards at times. Through physical and often emotional challenges, we become conditioned to not take risks for fear of loss or to avoid pain.

As I experience life, it is constantly challenging me and I am constantly faced with the decision to stop where I am at or to keep going. The challenge sometimes is to stay focused on the lessons and the potential opportunity for growth and achievement rather than the momentary pain or possible loss. I have been blessed with so many great experiences in life. Yet, as time goes by and bigger opportunities for growth emerge, I find myself needing to ask myself more and more if the end result will be worth it. *"Should I settle, or keep moving forward?"*

## "Life Is Good!"

Reflecting back and as I listen to one of the greatest groups of all time sing their song "September", I feel so inspired and filled with gratitude. The song by the nostalgic group Earth, Wind, & Fire starts with the rhythmically unique tempo and beat as the horns play in the song, the lead singer starts to sing the words with the reflective thought, "Do you remember, the 21st night in September..."

This was an incredible song that was to signal the beginning of a new life for me as I proudly walked down the aisle and out of the church with my ever so beautiful bride. I had actually facilitated and coordinated the music for literally hundreds of weddings before, but this one was special. This one was my very own! This was one of the best moments of my life! From that moment, I had been able to have so many wonderful experiences and adventures in life. If you have experienced true love and marry the person of your dreams, you know exactly what I am talking about. Who can ever forget their honeymoon and the wonderfully passionate nights that would be followed by having our own family and great friends? Life was good!

### "The Good, The Bad, & The Ugly"

Fast forward to today, where I am faced with the memories and reflections of those prior years which are so clear and vivid, but at the same time so blurred. I experienced so many blessings through marriage, being surrounded by numerous friends, and of course overcoming and learning from various family and personal challenges for many years. I thought I could withstand almost anything. Boy, was I wrong! I was confronted with the stark reality that my own life's course would be altered for the worse as issues would arise that we could not overcome. With a failing marriage and only a whisper of a relationship with God remaining, I needed to desperately come up with a solution. Well, I knew that my then-faithful wife's attitude and demeanor would eventually turn around. She is always able to boomerang back around, right? Not this time. I never really lost hope until I lost my wife. If you have experienced a significant separation through death or divorce, you understand the feelings and pain of loss.

Since then, I have reflected many times on what I had done wrong. Why was our marriage unable to survive the challenges we faced? I never had a "Plan B" for marriage, as it was never an option to have my own marriage fail. Thus, I was completely unprepared, caught off guard, and broadsided. Through many painful nights I sat in reflection, going through arguably the toughest, most relentless, and painful experience I had ever known. The pain was an emotional pain of separation and in this case, a loss of something that I held so dear not just from virtue but even from deeper within myself. Not only would it be a separation from my spouse, but a split of my family unit as a whole.

My way of dealing with things is not to isolate myself, but rather the opposite. Already an individual that always sought to serve others, this extremely devastating situation propelled me even further to help further "support the greater good", but I would now be doing it alone. For the most part, I haven't spent too much time looking back...but that was only after taking many good hard looks at my life. "What I could have done differently?" I asked myself, of course reflecting on the moment. I accepted the reality of the situation, also asking myself occasionally, "What just happened?"

After many sleepless nights of contemplation and trying to reach resolution with myself, I decided that this event in life was in some odd way to prepare me for something bigger and also help me truly not just understand, but empathize with those that go through what we call "LIFE". This situation, combined with helping serve my father, whose memory is failing at the time of this writing, has taught me so many valuable lessons. However, to reach these lessons, I needed to truly make some solid decisions and come to some very important conclusions for myself. I had always been one that has been able to help others "overcome", but now it was time to personally put into practice the advice and help that I had given to so many others. As the emotional barriers emerged, I needed to choose to continue to move forward. But would I be able to do it?

Dealing with the pain of separation is one of the most difficult things one can go through. My friend described separation by divorce as synonymous with "having someone die on you, only you get to see them over and over again and year after year - especially when kids are involved." I have always heard that when you become "single again", your primary friends change from married couples to people that have gone through the same thing. Wow! I can't explain it, but having had my primary close friendships with married couples, I find that today, much of my immediate demographics have indeed changed. Coping with the reality of the situation, it honestly was a very easy decision for me to truly decide to give wholeheartedly to others and help them reach their dreams. One thing I did realize, though, after a few years is that as my love for others increased, my love for myself decreased, which was not at all good or healthy. It no longer was at all about me, but entirely about others. I am sharing authentically and transparently, as I took this to an extreme and I literally removed myself from the equation.

After much reflection and consideration, I realized that the biggest mountain I needed to overcome was that of an emotional barrier. I needed to not let anything hold me back from restoring and loving myself! I am always still learning to make sure I actively love and value myself in everything I do. I truly understand more than ever that every moment we have is a blessing and that every breath we take while still on earth is a breath that no one else will have an opportunity to take. I do believe I have a fiduciary responsibility to never take for granted even a single breath.

From my experience and discussion with some experts dealing with grief and overcoming some emotional trauma of some major life situation, I realized that there are some key factors I needed to consider to help me work through those times to create the breakthroughs I wanted to achieve.

## KEYS TO BREAKING BARRIERS TO ACHIEVE GREATER THINGS

*Decide to love and forgive yourself and accept that life happens.*

This was a very important part of my starting to be able to feel good again. During these times, I started to look at situations and asked myself if I intentionally did anything wrong from my perspective. For me, I needed to verbalize the situation and actually say out loud many times, "I did the best I could at the time." It was a while until I accepted the situation, then had to deal with my own acceptance of myself and that **I DESERVED TO BE LOVED**. It eventually got to the point where I did forgive myself. This was not a single event, but a process to get to that point. Remember, **YOU DESERVE TO BE LOVED!**

*Understand that the healing is a process and not a single event.*

The irony of this point is that I am an active part of "Healings In Motion", a 10+ year non-profit dedicated to stroke awareness and brain health as well as caregiving. In the events, I get to participate and facilitate for this organization. We talk a considerable amount about healing. I didn't realize the emotional trauma people endured, whether it be a loss of a loved one through death or serving as a caregiver. Now being a part-time caregiver for my father and having gone through the separation with my ex-spouse, I understand how the wounds do not just instantaneously get better, but rather it is a continual process of healing. Knowing what to expect is one of the best things that has helped me be able to anticipate how things will be. I can then set up realistic expectations to heal. Healing is a journey and a process. Be kind and supportive to yourself on this journey.

*Surround yourself with some good friends that you know will be there for you.*

I am fortunate enough to be surrounded by people who are genuinely about helping others either through an organization they have formed or take an active part in helping others on a continual basis, either formally as a professional or as an involved volunteer. Many of these people have also experienced major life events that have made them stronger. They are people that I can always go to that truly know me and will listen, but also tell me the things I need to hear. They inspire me to keep going and I realize that I can do the same for others. Join, create, or look for a supportive community to walk with and beside you on the healing journey.

*Keep in mind why you are here.*

It definitely helps to remember that the challenges are difficult to overcome, but that there is a purpose to your life. There is a spark that you provide that will ignite the flame for someone else to be able to do something big. REMEMBER that you do matter and that your example and accomplishments can very well be the catalyst for something extraordinary to happen that may otherwise never emerge.

In summary, remember that you are here for a purpose. Enjoy the adventure of finding that purpose and then the excitement of accomplishing the things in life necessary for that purpose to be fulfilled. Remember that some barriers exist to protect, while others are there to be broken through. Without the challenges, we would never experience the excitement of accomplishment. Keep moving forward for your success and to achieve the greatness you deserve!

*"When Life Tries To Take You Down, Let The Experiences Become Lessons To Make You Stronger and Better."*

## MEET JIM T. CHONG...

Jim T. Chong is a Master Emcee and professional speaker, a licensed financial professional, and the founder of Solutions4Life, the Wok Star, and a radio personality in the Greater Sacramento area on MONEY 105.5 FM as the Wok Star on "Rush Hour For Success" and "Wok The Talk" on KXVS. He is also the founder of Catapult Media Production, a film making entity. Jim loves to help people achieve their personal aspirations and is actively involved and on the Executive Team of several established non-profit and cause-based communities and organizations in his local area. He excels in helping support those that wish to gain more influence and exposure in their local community by helping support them either as their Master Emcee, on the air waves, or through social media.

Jim supports and facilitates several workshops and programs such as the "Central Valley Recovery Awareness Preventing Strokes" (CV-RAPS) monthly program which is at St. Joseph's Medical Center in San Joaquin County on behalf of Healings In Motion (http://www.healingsinmotion.org) and also provides bi-monthly inspiration, personal development, and character/leadership talks for the Central Valley Asian American Chamber of Commerce IMC program and other organizations. Currently launching a movement called "Legacies, Legends, & Heroes" that is designed to help people awaken their story. Jim is a sought-after Master Emcee who has served as the Master Of Ceremonies to various established organizations and workshops and speaks in front of hundreds of people monthly.

He is the emcee of choice for the past several years for the Chinese New Year Parade in Stockton City, the Vietnamese Parade in Greater Sacramento that has thousands in attendance and also the Asian Festival in the town of Locke, California where he recently appeared on the national program for the Travel Channel in Ghost Adventures (http://www.locke-foundation.org). Jim has also helped produce award winning short films and is a co-owner of a theatre and entertainment company which gives a portion of its profits back to a designated cause.

Through the "Wok Star" personality, Jim is passionate about advancing culture, community, and commerce by establishing collaborative venues and is looking forward to the launch of his global radio show "Live Strong America-Radio To Inspire" and is currently launching "The CEO Leadership Corner" with Jon Taber. He gets his fulfillment supporting the greater good by helping individuals' dreams come true by developing strategies for their money, message, and moments in life.

### *Contact Information for Jim T. Chong:*

Direct:    925.860.9777
Email:    jtc.wokstar@gmail.com

# GET UP, GET OVER IT, GET GOING!
## By Elena Crandell

*Can you relate to the relief one feels
after the hustle and bustle of bag check-in,
long security lines, walking to your gate,
and finally boarding the plane?*

If you're like me, I always dread the tedious and tiring process of flying. Similarly, the skies of life can be calm and clear or dark and stormy, leaving us physically and emotionally exhausted.

I was born in Colombia, where I was raised by my grandparents and where I spent my childhood. Life was simple until my teen years, when I moved to the U.S. The chaos within the walls of my new home became so unbearable that I decided to quit school and leave home at the age of sixteen. Being on my own without life experience, street smarts, and working skills was difficult, to say the least. Somehow through my faith in God, I got the courage to do what I needed to do to get by. A year later I met the man who became my husband for twenty-nine years and with whom I had three beautiful daughters. Fast forward to today, three decades later, I'm once again facing the dark and stormy skies of life, now dealing divorce, learning a new set of skills, and finding a new career. Just like then, I have no choice but to "Get Up, Get Over It, and Get Going" with my life.

I recently traveled to Miami and after the airplane reached cruising altitude, I gladly settled and went into relaxation mode. Then the much-dreaded jerking movements caused by air turbulence began. As the airplane jerked again and again, the captain's voice came on over the speaker and announced, "Ladies and gentlemen, we are experiencing unexpected turbulence. Please take your seats and fasten your seatbelts." As the turbulence intensified, people began to panic. My palms began to sweat, my heart to race, and thoughts of the unthinkable invaded my mind. I started to feel terror and it was then that I felt I had to do something. I realized I had two choices: to panic like everyone else, or to stay calm. Although in reality the turbulence only lasted a few minutes, it seemed to have lasted a lifetime. Turbulence in the air is part of nature, whether we like it or not. Even with modern radar and weather predicting equipment, airplanes are subject to the effects of rough wind currents. As a passenger, there isn't much we can do, but the pilot can. He can make course corrections, decide to go through it, or he can choose to divert the plane to another location if there's threat to safety. Just like the scenario in the airplane, I was going through dark and cloudy storms from the ages of thirteen to sixteen. I didn't know I was the pilot of my plane and that I had choices until turbulence in my life became so intense that I instinctively decided to divert to another location.

**GET UP!**

Compare, Despair, Impair have been my constant companions throughout my life. I have come to a conclusion and realization that no-one is perfect and no-one is good at everything. Comparing ourselves to others leaves us discouraged and robs us of focusing on our God-given callings, talents, and destinies. I've learned that all I can do to be the better version of myself is to be at peace with who I am. The Bible tells us in John 16:33, "I have told you these things, so that in Me you may have peace. In this world you will have trouble. But take heart! I have overcome the world." It's true that some people will like you for who you are, most will like you for what you can do for them, and some will not like you at all, but God intentionally created us just the way we are meant to be and He will always have our backs! Don't allow other people to determine what you want and don't let their comments or opinions get to you. This puts your hopes and dreams at risk of being tossed and blown in the wind's negative influence. We must ignore naysayers and surround ourselves with "yes"-sayers, people who make us feel good, who believe in us and want only the best for us. The next time life's turbulences knock the wind out of you, remember to "Get Up, Get Over It and Get Going". This will be a sure way to break through the turbulence and clouds of adversity.

Are you experiencing turbulence right now? You have options: deal with it or stay in it. When you are cruising along life and you experience sudden turbulence, a good question to ask yourself is, "What can I do now or how am I going to handle this situation?" If you were the pilot of the plane, would you say, "I can't decide what to do; I'm too scared. I'll deal with this later?" How would that help the situation? If you are able to take immediate action, do it. Take control of your own responses and reactions and choose to not have a mob mentality. Mob mentality describes how people are influenced by their peers or people around them to adopt certain behavior or responses, such as the case in my travel experience. I could have chosen to panic, but I chose to take control of my own responses.

When facing turbulences, we can choose to surrender to the circumstance, accept the circumstance, or shift gears and move on. We can't always control the frequency or intensity of turbulence life sends our way. We may feel shaken, blown about by the turbulence of disappointment, doubt, fear, devastation, sadness or even stress. How we ride the turbulence out will be the key determining factor in our outcome. We can use adversity as a stepping stone or a millstone. The difference is that one moves us up to greater understanding and growth and the other weighs us down, keeping us from getting up, getting over things, and moving forward. The difference between up in the air turbulence and turbulence in our everyday life is who's in control. In our own lives, we are the pilot. We have the ability to choose the appropriate course of action. As much as we don't like the effects of turbulence in our lives, they can be good for us because they bring about change.

Here are some degrees of turbulence we may experience:

- *Bumps* which can slow us down

- *Jolting or shaking* which can put fear in us

- *Life-threatening* events which take courage to get through

- *Catastrophes* which require time and attention to heal

So you get hit with turbulence...what do you do? Here are some helpful steps to follow:

1) Take a deep breath. Stay calm.

2) Ask yourself, "What's happening?" What exactly is the turbulence or problem ?

3) Ask yourself, "What can I do now? Am I in control of this situation?" (you'll find that most of the time you're not)

4) Ask yourself, "What is my reaction going to be?: (panic versus staying calm)

I've always told my daughters Andrea, Monica, and Kayla to stay "CCC" (Calm, Cool and Collected) whenever they left the house and they've never forgotten it.

5) Give yourself a **soft landing**. Life can be intense. Don't you wish a warning sign would come on saying "hold on; turbulence ahead?" Things don't always work the way we want them to. People change. Our kids grow up and move away, we can lose our jobs, our marriages, our best friends.

6) Count your blessings and name them *one by one*, as a hymn well put it. When we are experiencing turbulence, it's easy to forget about all that is going well. Be mindful to remember and think about all your blessings. I always tell my girlfriends that the antidote to sadness is gratitude. Writing down what is going right and what we are grateful for is helpful in getting us through the dark, stormy clouds of life. The goal is to live each moment for what it is, no matter how bad it appears. Diverting from reality and resisting it only results in more suffering. Creating a soft landing for yourself will take practice and effort. Remember that your current state of mind is only temporary and that circumstances change. Most of us have compassion for others, but struggle with not having compassion for ourselves, which can in turn help minimize our anxiety, insecurity, and lack of self-love. Just as it is onboard an airplane – breaking through the clouds brings sighs of relief and the ability to breathe easier.

**GET OVER IT!**

Stop looking back and start bouncing back! Zig Ziglar said, "When you focus on your problems, you get more problems, and when you focus on possibilities, you have more opportunities." Don't allow past failures to define your worth. If you look back at history, you will find that all stories of great success are also stories of great triumph over adversity. Such was the case with Thomas Edison, who failed 10,000 times before he succeeded with the light bulb. He famously said, "I never failed. I just found 10,000 ways that wouldn't work." It was also his belief that "Many of life's failures are people who *gave up too soon*." The Bible tells us in Isaiah 43:18, "Forget what happened in the past, and do not dwell on events from long ago." I have personally come to believe that if we want our lives to be an amazing story, we must begin by realizing that God is the author of it and every day He gives us the opportunity to participate in the writing of each new page. Admitting mistakes and forgiving others shows humility, maturity, and is an admirable act of courage. Refusing to allow setbacks and failures to define us and choosing to rise again and again is what propels us to move forward and get over whatever it is that is holding us back. Find your niche, your calling, and your passion. Refuse to let life's unpredictable turbulences keep you from your destiny because no one but God knows you like you know yourself. **<u>Break through the Barriers</u>** of adversity and *Get Up, Get Over It, and Get Going.* Your future awaits you!

## GET GOING!

I have been a fitness instructor many, many, years and have been around people long enough to understand how hard it is to start a fitness routine, and especially how hard it is to have it interrupted or end due to illness, injury, or disruption from the busyness of life. Re-establishing a routine again takes determination and commitment. Instead of thinking about how tiring exercise can be, or how challenging it will be to fit working out into your schedule, focus on how good you'll look and how awesome you will feel in the long run. By focusing on one goal at a time, we prevent overloading ourselves and we can better maintain energy and focus. Strengthen your resolve to pursue a rigorous routine - whatever that is to you - and stick to the plan. Build, tone, and improve the muscles in your life. I like to get inspiration from people who have achieved what I want to achieve, or who are currently in the process of reaching their goals. I enjoy reading my Bible for guidance, hope, and inspiration, and I read books and blogs that open and broaden my mind and attend personal growth seminars. Think now of your goals and dreams and approach those as you would a long journey. Don't give up with every little bump, but stay focused on them for the long term, ride out the ebbs and surf on the flows. Build on the small successes and celebrate the benefits of your accomplishments because they will fuel and energize you. Most importantly, remember to **call on the One Who Calms the Storm. The Bible says** in Isaiah 40:31, *"But they that wait upon the Lord shall renew their strength; they shall mount up with wings as eagles, they shall run, and not be weary; and they shall walk, and not faint."* Use the power God has given you to **Get Up, Get Over It, and Get Going!**

Take action. Your life depends on it!

## MEET ELENA CRANDELL...

Elena Crandell is a Colombian native, and U.S. Citizen who has lived in California for the past thirty years. She a blessed mom of three beautiful young adult, kind-hearted daughters. Elena is a piano teacher, and a licensed Esthetician.

Elena was also a Fitness Professional and a Spanish Enrichment Teacher at the local elementary and middle schools. She created a movement called Fitkidsmove and is an energetic, passionate individual, who is committed to serving the local communities by serving the homeless through various projects throughout the year. She has planned, organized and executed several fundraisers to benefit cancer patients, prevention of human trafficking and the provision of clean water well projects in various third world countries.

Elena is a people person who enjoys meaningful fellowship and gets involved in all aspects of group interaction throughout the community and has acted as Master of Ceremonies (MC) at many corporate, community and personal events. When asked, people would describe Elena unanimously, as a woman with a big heart, full of kindness and life of the party. Elena describes herself as a woman of Faith and a life-learner.

# EVERYONE CAN REACH THEIR DREAMS
## By Dr. Julie Damron-Brown

Overcoming obstacles is never easy. This sounds trite, but if it was easy, everyone would be successful and living their dreams. Many are working in jobs they don't like just to pay the bills, wishing they had made different life choices. Others are worried about taking chances. Barriers can be created by unexpected life events and/or we can also allow our own personal fears to build walls. Everyone can reach their dreams. There are some key strategies to making an ambition a reality.

My childhood was not a fairytale. Enough said. I grew up feeling very alone as an only child in a single parent household. I decided at the age of five that I wanted to be a veterinarian. If there is one thing that helped me though all the challenges of life, it was my determination and belief that I could achieve this goal. My persistence allowed me to ignore the barrage of naysayers who felt perpetually obligated to sound their advice. It allowed me to push forward through nine years of college study in biology, physiology, organic chemistry, calculus, genetics, and more.

And now as I look back at my over twenty-year career as a female veterinarian in what was once a field dominated mostly by men (many veterinary schools didn't allow women initially), I embrace all of the challenges that I faced and celebrate them. They made me fight even harder and gave so much more meaning to what I have achieved at this time. I am not only currently the medical director for The Stockton Veterinary Emergency and Specialty Center, the writer of a bi-monthly pet health column in *The Record* since 2007, the on-air show host for The Voice of Stockton KXVS Radio's weekly broadcast program Tails and Tips, but also a 2017-2018 Don Lowe Fellow at the UC Davis School of

Veterinary Medicine in the specialty area of Emergency Medicine and Critical Care.

Additionally, I am a very strong community advocate, and am currently running for San Joaquin County Board of Supervisors. I co-founded the Delta Veterinary Medical Association - a group that provides continuing education and other support for veterinarians in our community. I am the current vice president. I have established a free vaccine clinic, Loving Tails, for the animals of the homeless that rotates on a monthly basis at four different locations throughout Stockton. I am a member of The Rotary Club of Stockton, and the first Vice President for The Stockton Hosts Lions. I serve on the board for The Stockton Emergency Food Bank, Pixie Woods, HOPE (Helping Other People to Expand), and I am an alternate for The Disabled American Veterans Charities of San Joaquin. I assist at least ten other additional nonprofits including Junior League and The United Way. I am on The Hunger Task Force, The Homeless Task Force, and a member of The American Legion Karl Ross Post 16 Auxiliary. I am an active member of The Stockton Chamber of Commerce, Hispanic Chamber, Asian Chamber, and am an Ambassador for Toys for Tots, a Stockton Chamber Ambassador, as well as a Certified Tourism Ambassador for The City of Stockton.

Having goals is paramount for success. At least for me, a goal provided a beacon or guiding light of where I was going, what I was trying to achieve. As with any goal, the next step is rigorous investigation. This allows one to explore if what they think they want to achieve is actually doable and truly desirable or a good fit for them. Many students attend UC Davis as an undergraduate with the hopes of entering veterinary school. At least seventy percent change their minds within the first two years, after they experience the joys of learning about chemistry with 500 of their closest friends and other difficulties.

Be a life learner. Continually seek out new and more information. Knowledge is the key to planning goals and determining a path to achieve them. Information helps you to formulate new ideas and look at things from many different perspectives. Formal education is never a waste of time and will only help you advance. Many jobs only let you move up so far without a college degree.

Keep an open mindset. Realize that there are always new and better ways to do things. Listen to others and how they have accomplished what they have, and what they are doing. The more you are aware of what is going on in the world and your community, the more of an active role you can play to be a beacon for change. Participate in as many community events and clubs as possible. Affiliate with the movers and shakers in your community. They are often found in service clubs such as Rotary, city Chamber groups, and on non-profit boards.

Devote your time only to things you really care about. Your passion will carry you through the difficulties. I only participate in organizations or events that are meaningful to me and when I participate, I go full throttle. It is true that showing up is half the battle, but you have to do more than just sit there to really be a part of something great, something that changes lives or changes our world for the better. And when you do go to events, always look professional and have your game face on. You have no idea what connections you can make at any time or place.

Mentors or guides are essential! They are great sources of information and support. Finding one or two people that are doing what you want to do, or have knowledge about some chosen area, can be the difference between success and failure. Such people can help you to avoid common pitfalls and give direction on how you can realize your dreams. Observe them as much as possible. See how they command authority. See how they lead people. See how they support others. Watch how they act in a crisis. Envision yourself in all of these roles. How will your techniques differ? How will you develop your own leadership style?

The next step is breaking up the goal into multiple steps. These bite-sized mini chunks allow you to move incrementally towards the objective in a manageable fashion. Almost anything is doable when divided into small tasks. Tiny advances are not scary. And with each achievement, one's confidence grows. Make sure to celebrate each victory, no matter how small. Remember, each triumph brings you that much closer to your ultimate desired destiny.

There has to be a plan to tackle any goal. For me, I like to have plan A, B, C, and D as a way to achieve something. This gives me flexibility and options. If it turns out that something cannot be reached by using one technique, it doesn't derail me. The realization that there are many ways to accomplish the same thing is pivotal. So many are halted in their tracks at the first barrier. Others let the fear of something paralyze them into inaction. Many believe that action is risky; however, there is also great risk with doing nothing.

In between these steps there is analysis, regrouping, and recovery. Is your strategy working? Do you need to adjust anything? Is it time for a time out? It is essential to have recuperative time, even if it is just taking a nap. A fresh perspective can make a world of difference with strategy. Rest is paramount for clear thinking. Exercise is also critical for me. It helps me to destress, unwind, and regroup. It physically, mentally, and emotionally feeds my soul. Touch base with your mentors and if your mentors do not support you, find different ones that do. But remember, you must be your strongest advocate. Only you can do the work to achieve your dream.

Plan for failure. If you are not having bumps in the road, then you are either the most amazing person ever, you are not being honest, or you are not challenging yourself. Experiencing pitfalls is an integral part of building success. Breaking barriers is working through these obstacles and coming out on the other side a champion. I was rejected the first time I applied for veterinary school. I also had to repeat one of my board exams during my senior year. I share this because it is reality. No matter how hard you work or try, there will be times you do not initially succeed. There is nothing wrong with that as long as you do not let it stop you.

See it, feel it, taste it. Become it before you achieve it. If you don't believe you can do it, no one else will! I can't stress this enough. You have to be your own best advocate and fight for what you want. Be prepared to explain why you deserve what you want and how you are uniquely qualified to be at whatever position you desire. Have your five minute elevator speech prepared so that you can explain what you want to do to anyone at any time at anyplace at the drop of a hat. You need to express yourself and act with confidence, as if you have been doing this chosen role your entire life. Walk with power. Command authority. Confidence gets you everywhere.

Life is short; savor every minute. Make sure you take time to enjoy your life. Not to sound cliché, but tomorrow is promised to no one. One does not want to regret missing out on certain things. Having said that, any endeavor will require some level of sacrifice. Each individual has to create a balance of work and play that makes sense to him or her. Do not be so focused on your destination that you forget to enjoy the salient points of the journey.

Giving back to the community is paramount. Helping others highlights the miracles that occur in life on a daily basis. There is so much that is amazing, if you only open your eyes to see it. When you assist those in need, it makes the impossible seem possible. It sustains and rejuvenates your heart. It also helps to keep your ego in check. It lets you realize that your daily problems and concerns are really not that significant in comparison to what many in our community are going through, and to appreciate what you have.

These last two concepts also tie in with being grateful. Although you may not be in the position that you want to be, be thankful for what you have. So many people have nothing. Within my adopted home town of Stockton, so many live below the poverty line. Remember that no matter what challenges you are facing, there are others that are struggling as well.

Please keep in mind that you can always change what is going on in your life at any time. Please remember that no one has gotten to where they are on their own. Know that even though it seems that things come easily to others, there is a lot of ground work that takes place to achieve anything. Do not worry about what others are doing and do not compare yourself to them. Just strive to be the best that you can be. Be yourself. Do what you say you will. Be amazing. And most importantly, never forget that anything is possible, and never give up!

## MEET DR. JULIE DAMRON-BROWN...

Dr. Julie Damron-Brown has been a veterinarian in the community for over twenty years. She is currently the medical director for Stockton Veterinary Emergency and Specialty Center. Her undergraduate and graduate degrees are from UC Davis School of Veterinary Medicine, where she currently has a Fellowship in Emergency Medicine and Critical Care.

She has a bi-monthly pet column in *The Stockton Record* and a weekly radio show on The Voice of Stockton. She is a very strong community advocate, a member of The Rotary Club of Stockton and the first Vice President of the Stockton Hosts Lions. She is also a member of The Woman's Auxiliary at Karl Ross Post 16, Leadership Stockton 2017, The Stockton Chamber of Commerce, The Hispanic Chamber, and The Asian Chamber; as well as an Ambassador for Toys for Tots, a Certified Tourism Ambassador, and a Chamber Ambassador. She serves on The Homeless and Hunger Tasks Forces and is a board member for The Emergency Food Bank, HOPE, and Pixie Woods. Julie founded a clinic called Loving Tails that provides free vaccines and other services to the animals of the homeless and low income on a monthly basis, rotating at four locations throughout Stockton. She strongly supports our local veterans and has chaired The Inaugural Patriot's Ball.

She is currently running for San Joaquin County Board of Supervisors because she wants to make a difference. She is concerned about protecting our county's quality of life. There are many issues facing our county, and she wants to be a part of the solution by working with others to find common ground, and creating opportunities for our community members. Her background as a doctor makes her uniquely qualified in understanding how to address multiple issues simultaneously as well as triaging to prioritize the most critical issues.

### *Contact Information for Dr. Julie Damron-Brown:*

Email:      purplejulied@yahoo.com

Facebook:   Julie Damron-Brown

# RED LIGHT/GREEN LIGHT INTUITION
## *By Cliff DeBaugh*

I watched in agony as the U-Haul pulled away, repeating to myself with an anguished scream inside my car, "Noooooooooooooooooo" in one long breath. I descended into a dark, empty, hollow space created deep in my soul as the truck slowly moved out of sight. I sat stunned by the turn of events that had happened over the last eight months. From somewhere deeper I heard, "How do we get through this?"

It was now all gone: wife, children (actually teenagers), furniture, and a relationship of almost twenty years, all within eight months. Who would have thought a minor traffic accident would have an effect this devastating in such a short time when it wasn't my fault - as if assigning blame had any real value? My injury was a severe concussion from being rear ended at a stoplight.

I was left with no past memories, the inability to remember anything recent, an inability to carry on a conversation, no sense of taste or smell, the inability to do math and repeat simple phrases, and a mild headache 24/7. Damn.

While I didn't realize it at the time, that amazing, wonderful, beautiful accident completely changed my life. While at the accident scene, the EMTs asked if I was okay. I answered, "Yes, but my head hurts and I'm a little dizzy." So they had me sit down while attending to the lady who hit me. According to them, I was doing fine. Well, according to me, I wasn't. I walked into walls at my next stop. I completely missed doorways, forgot what I was doing there, and also repeated myself. After driving 40 miles back to the warehouse, I finally went to the ER and the doctor gave me Tylenol with codeine to relieve the pain.

What I didn't know was how my body would react to these added chemicals to my now freshly-injured brain, which was producing its own chemical blend to heal my mind. To put it simply, it was not good! After three days, I started yelling at the slightest noise, yelling about noises echoing, and pounding inside my head. My wife actually threw the pills at me after an outburst, saying, "It's either the pills or me." Well, I chose her at the time, but later she would not choose me. Oh well...so it goes.

About two months after this amazing turn of events, my wife sat me down on the couch and calmly told me she was moving – well, she and the kids were. I wasn't. In my condition, I didn't understand. She was moving and I was not, but we had been together twenty years, so what did she mean? I really didn't "get it". I said, "Okay, I'll find a place."

"Oh, hey," she said, "you can keep the cat."

As I looked back over those eight months after I settled into my new apartment, I experienced the loneliness of recovery with no visible injury. The pressure inside my head often led to another headache on top of the one I constantly had, making day-to-day life unbearable inside my small space. I just wanted relief. Sometimes crying from severe pain relieved my tension as further benefits were elusive. During those times, I would reflect back on the whole situation, realizing how crazy life had turned out to be. I also discovered there was a certain solace in thinking within my body, a peaceful calm in the quiet.

I was an optimist who was not supported by my partner in life. We had more ups than downs in our twenty years. I realized that if I was influenced by my wife into negative outcomes, then by having confidence in myself to be wholly positive, I could have all the goodness I could handle and negative situations would be minimal. I wanted joy and happiness from here on, even with a headache. I didn't know how, except someplace deeper I heard, "Keep going."

Shortly after moving, I found a group of people who were positive, motivated, and caring, and a training program to teach about life. Nope, it was not a church, but a network marketing company*. I was shocked as I enjoyed the company of motivated, positive people who were looking to make a change in the world for future generations. I had changed my environment, which would change my life. The company also had products that would eventually heal my brain!

Since my concussion was a work-related injury, I was subject to unannounced doctor's appointments as well as scheduled ones. I could not miss any or my claim could be delayed or cancelled. The doctors wanted to give me "mind candy" (heavy drugs) which were later deemed illegal to prescribe. I refused, instead touting my positive attitude and natural products. Their outlook was let them be the doctors while mine was "I'm the patient, it's my body, what are the side effects?" Within myself, I could hear that voice more clearly, now saying to me, "Danger...danger."

I politely told the doctors I would continue what I was doing, as the products I were using were 100% natural as described by the manufacturer, exactly the way they were describing the drugs - except I could not overdose nor take too much, since my body would throw off any excess. The company's products were of great assistance in my recovery and I use them to this day.

What I figured out was that during situations either with doctors or stressful uncertainties of day-to-day life, I had this inner knowing. All I know is that as long as I listened to my inner voice, everything was okay. I was learning to live in the moment.

As to where I was in life, I was diagnosed with 40% loss of cognitive ability according to a number of tests. I could not remember anything; I would get internally angry at myself for knowing I could do a task before the accident, however now I couldn't remember how to do that same task. That would leave me totally frozen in place from stress until I relaxed. This proved embarrassing, so I learned to laugh to relieve tension so I wouldn't be a statue in the middle of a room.

What had happened to me? This was not a good position to try and piece life back together to rebuild a future. At that time, future meant the next minute, next hour, or next day, nothing further, as the continuing headache was ever present. Looking back, at a previous job I did home delivery of food and ice cream to over 150 homes a day. I remembered routes, names, dogs' names, kids' names, the cars my customers drove, their schedules, their favorite flavors, everything about them on a two week cycle. There were fifteen hundred homes on the route cycle. And now I couldn't repeat a simple sentence back to you after hearing it or drive a freeway and know which off ramps to take. I would fight off anxiety while trying to make a decision. During those times, I would hear the voice trying to calm me down.

As events unfolded, I met a beautiful woman who would become my lifelong friend. We supported each other, as she also was recovering from a major life event. Our relationship lasted through three years of discovery, personal growth, and love for each other. We are friends and love each other as friends to this day, for which I am extremely grateful.

Fast forward five years. Life is progressing and I have slowly learned to work independently as a service merchandiser in the San Joaquin valley. I get paid by the task, not the hour so I don't have a direct boss or time clock. When I turn in paperwork, I get paid. My headache still pushes against my skull every day 24/7. At least until the day comes when I have relief, I can work. I know I have got to get rid of this, as it limits my recovery.

By chance, friends asked me if I wanted to go to the Chinese Lantern Festival in San Francisco, so I went. At the event, we came across a Qi Gong master direct from China. A ten minute treatment was $10. I explained through a translator what hurt, and his reply was, "Okay, three times come." I got treated and we returned to the city the next two days as well. I was feeling some relief after day two. On day three the master puts me on his back, picked me up, shook me briskly, and dropped me to the ground on very wobbly legs. I was stunned into good health as my headache disappeared after five years. Wow!

Life evolved in many ways as I changed jobs to the recycling industry, experienced international travel, and worked without being paid September 2001 to January 2002 (thanks 9/11). I experienced gratitude for the ability to not worry about money, knowing the universe was taking care of me. With this company, I have time to look back on the last seven years, reflecting on how far I have progressed since November '94. I have gained so much as I pay attention to my internal voice. I am calm, and I have a more outgoing personality. I'm happy being me, I have confidence in my abilities, and I understand the larger impact of small change on the planet through the employers' environmental message.

Most importantly, I'm learning to apply the life lessons of my recovery process. As I have taken these lessons forward, I entered fields I knew nothing about, gained knowledge, and became self-employed in the fireplace industry. I service wood burning pellet stoves during the winter. It is not glamorous; however, I meet all types of people from all walks of life in their homes. I work alone; my day is mine. I have learned to listen to my inner voice while assessing different issues regarding a stove's performance. That voice is always looking out for me no matter where I am.

From 2004 to present day, this is my "job". It's not my dream; however, it does give me time to think about the future I'm creating. Something out of all this pain, continual recovery, observation and accumulated knowledge has brought me to what I see as my new future, a future where I also get to work daily with joy and gratitude, even if it's as little as sending an email or as much as attending an event to promote our message. Small actions amount to making a large accomplishment over time.

The company I started is named Ready4Rescue. Our mission statement is "Giving life a second chance, when seconds count". Our goal is to reduce 911 response time in the home. We prepare your home, your information, and you before you make a 911 call. It is a proactive approach. It can be lifesaving to be ready for the small emergencies that may occur in the home on a day-to-day basis.

Our team has been working on this for three years, putting our system together. We have been testing our message about 911 readiness. What we know is that it's working. People have not thought about this part of home emergency preparation. A small emergency when unprepared could be a disaster for a family, as statistics show a family could lose as much as 60% of the family income from a medical emergency.

We have products to help locate your home at night. These products reduce anxiety of being found when visibility and landmarks disappear under the cover of darkness. We use existing protocols coupled with technology. It's an exciting place to be, creating a system that will save lives.

What gets me through the day are the people I meet, either in their homes or at a business conference. I find it fascinating to ask a question of a person and listen with my mind and my heart as I hear the truth about their family, their experiences, or their life circumstances. Everyone has a different story, no matter the culture. In listening to so many, I have discovered we are all very much alike in so many ways. Our differences come into play, as our cultural traditions are ingrained so deeply. We may fail to see our neighbors as equals, yet they have the same issues as anyone else with a different cultural understanding. Our neighbors have the same crazy uncle, doddering grandma, divorced parents, car accidents, recovering aging parents, or yippy dog as others in our family. There is no difference, only different cultures looking at life through their own upbringing and societal guidelines.

So since the accident and with over 20+ years passing - which seems like the blink of an eye - I have overcome many things that appear normal from my point of view. It happens to all of us. What got me through the ups and downs was a positive point of view, staying in the moment, not getting rattled or angry, surrounding myself with people who are moving forward in life, and having fun in whatever I do. I think the one most important lesson is to listen to my inner voice. I think it's my soul reaching out to keep me on track to make change in the world. As I found out earlier, a small voice can make many ripples. Find YOUR voice and you will be amazed as to what will transpire.

## MEET CLIFF DeBAUGH...

Cliff DeBaugh's work career has encompassed many areas of commerce from retail sales, commercial route sales, breaking new advertising ground introducing trivia slides at the movies, home delivery route sales of frozen food and ice cream, sales crew leader for residential sales of a leading water company, wholesale coffee service to offices and industry, survived a major concussion (40% loss of cognitive abilities), self-employment as a freelance merchandiser/reset specialist traveling the western United States.

During the early 2000's Cliff has also worked in the plastic recycling industry working as personal assistant to the CEO, later moving to project coordinator/government liaison. Building on this experience Cliff later worked in operations for a fluorescent light recycler. Both of these companies gave Cliff an introduction to international travel.

Leaving the recycling field Cliff married, started working in the wholesale building materials industry importing magnetic doorstops for commercial and retail stores. This business led to inventing an address identifying blue light for emergency responders to find homes quicker.

As life changed Cliff divorced, moving to Stockton/Lodi to learn about the fireplace industry while employed at a retail store, moving into installation and service of wood burning pellet stoves. He recently attained certification with the Air Pollution Control District to inspect and certify pellet/wood burning appliances as clean burning, issuing a certificate valid for three years to the homeowner.

Doubling efforts with the stove business Cliff worked on his passion of reducing 911 response times in the home. Using his experience of being in over 10,000 homes during his career, Cliff invented a system to make the home more visible, with ready information and preparedness calling it Ready4Rescue.

Ready4Rescue will assist residents to be ready BEFORE making a 911 call relieving the caller of anxiety, frustration and worry. Also to assist the homeowner, Ready4Rescue has released a web-app to provide the homeowner with an easy to use home inspection to increase awareness about delays outside and inside the home. Since information is critical in an emergency Ready4Rescue has released its second web-app enabling the home owner to carry personal health information with them wherever they go. Currently Cliff is at the early start-up stage of the business while seeking funding to expand Ready4Rescue into a known entity locally, regionally, and nationally.

### *Contact Information for Cliff DeBaugh:*

Email:          info@ready4rescue.com

Phone:          (209)663-3678

Website:        www.ready4rescue.com

# A FATHER/DAUGHTER JOURNEY:
## A DESIRE TO CHANGE AND ALTER YOUR LIFE
### Excerpt on: Philip Duncan
#### By Leanna Wolff (Daughter)

**June 24, 1976**

On the frame of my 1974 Raleigh Competition racing bike I pedaled on through the sweltering heat. My two spare tires were spinning steadily in rhythm with the spiral of pessimistic thinking that was in fact the truth of the situation. My stomach chimed in and growled in sync with my thoughts. Although I had very little water left, no food, no spare tires, and no money, somehow the saddles on my bicycle began to sit heavier onto my frame, as if they were gathering the weight of the circumstances as well. No longer able to power through, I slowed my pedaling and the sound of the chomping gravel that had already blown my original tires made me cringe as I coasted to the shoulder.

Ponderosa pine trees infused the hot air and the horizon held nothing more than ceaseless hills with a single passage running through it like a metal ladle that had been sitting in a heated pot too long. But I could no longer see the surrounding beauty, just the single square foot of shaded pavement that my own fetal shadow had given birth to on this lonely, hot road. A rush of tears began to litter the asphalt and dried almost instantly in the 105 degree temperatures. They came freely, knowing there was no one to see for miles and in that moment, I had never felt more alone in my fifteen years of life. Just under 400 miles in and over 3,850 to go, I had every reason to bike into the next small town, find a payphone and use my last dime to call my parents and call it quits.

It would take ten days of riding and over 600 miles to the next Western Union where a wire transfer would hopefully be waiting for me (the last one had not), but how would I make it that far on just these two thin racing tires with no spares, nothing to eat, and no cash to buy either of these necessities? Despair had not only set in, it had taken over, and I knew I had to make a decision whether or not to abandon this dream.

At just fifteen years of age, in the summer of 1976, Philip Duncan was an average student, a distance runner, outgoing, and the younger brother to his taller, tougher twin. It was the 200 year anniversary of the country and the 100 year anniversary of the invention of the bicycle so the Bikecentennial Trans-America Ride was born. Driven by his dream to see the country firsthand (yet ironically not even old enough to drive a car) he made a life-altering decision to ride his bicycle across the United States of America. It took some coercing to get his parents to agree to such an expedition, and while it began with a friend who was eighteen (and therefore so much older and wiser), his parents agreed. So with his twenty-three pound racing bike - a now laughable "light-weight" model - and a pannier saddle pack hugging its rear frame brimming with field guides and maps, a pup tent, a sleeping bag, a stove, a water bottle, and far too many clothes, he caught a ride from Sacramento California up to Reeds Port, Oregon and the journey began. He didn't know what he did not know and before he got through the first state of Oregon, he was on his own in every sense of the word.

There comes a time in the course of your life that you realize the goal you have set may be bigger and more challenging than you are up for tackling. The signs all seem to say "Stop", "Road Closed", or as Google maps now likes to cheerily inform us, "Make a U-Turn, if possible". This was my father's defining moment that set the course for the rest of his life. It paved the road of determination in my own life and as I encountered obstacles over the years, my resolve never to lose sight of my dreams - which he had so clearly defined - was a constant source of inspiration. An infectious inspiration that I hope brings clarity and courage towards a limitless future for my own daughters.

### April 17, 2000

It's been one month since that fateful day. Thick corduroy snow coated the mountain runs and reflected the suns radiant energy. It glittered with the same effervescence that was coursing through my body as I rode the chair lift to the top in my designer gear, blond braided pigtails jutting out in the periphery of my goggle lenses. The park was beautiful that day and I had my eyes on the biggest jump there. At about 20' tall with a 15' tabletop I had already landed each of my nine jumps with ease. The rush I got each time was addictive and this time I was going to see just how big I could go. As I heard the last click of my binding tighten to performance, I pushed myself to a standing position and took off on my well-thought-out plan of execution. Without taking a single turn, gaining every sliver of speed the slope of the mountain would allow before I could take that launch, I was unstoppable. And fifteen.

As soon as my board shot past the front lip of the jump, I was catapulted into the air. The speed was instantly more than I could pilot and although connected, my board and body were no longer on the same mission. It began to rise above my head and in that same time-idled moment, I looked to my right to see the faces of three people riding up the chair lift. Although all I could hear was my own heartbeat, I heard their words as clear as the ones playing out in my head..."o-h-h s-h-i—i-t . . ." We were parallel, this chair and I, which meant I had to be at least forty feet in the air, a passenger on a plane that was going down. I knew in that moment this could be the end of my story.

To this day, it is as surreal as having an out of body experience, one that you know you were there for but you still can't figure out how you lived through it. The same way your iPhone can now cinematically slow down and stretch a ten second moment into a minute, that scene somehow played out in just the same way as I was suspended in both time and air the moment I took lift off. As soon as my curled spine hit hard-packed snow - twenty feet past the end of slope that should have eased me back to earth - I didn't feel the immediate pain that ensued because all I could think about was confirming I could still feel my fingers and toes. I could. *Then* came the screaming between great gasps of air because if you've ever had the wind knocked out of you...well, it was reminiscent of that but amplified beyond comparison. I managed to break four vertebrae, and miraculously, none of those fractures severed my spinal cord.

After weeks of living in a borrowed reclining leather throne that decorated our living room, hedged with pillows that tried to relieve the perpetual pain, I began to feel more in tune with the pulse of life than ever before. As the visitors and so-called "best friends" had flowed in early on to show their love and support, the floodgates quickly ceased to see a mere trickle. I can't imagine it was easy to witness my stranded situation and the obvious pain I was in, and they had their own lives to attend to. Then there was just my mother. She pulled me through it, helping feed, clothe, bathe, and hold me when the pain was too much to bear. I realized just how breakable I was, how quickly life could take an alternate route, and how much I had left to accomplish in this life...and in this same body. Prior to the accident I had a time-honored teenage relationship with my mother, but then my whole world shifted. Trivial matters of social status, looks, and coasting through life took the backseat to meaningful relationships, compassion for others, and a laser focus on my goals.

I don't live a day without being grateful for how differently my life could have played out. Once I could get back to school, I put all of my efforts into excelling so that I could go to a great college and continue on to live my childhood dream of becoming a famous architect. Well, I had to make several adjustments along the way because things don't always go according to plan...or rather we can't plan for what we don't know. I completed a two year degree in just a year with honors so I could transfer to the Art Institute. After graduating at the top of my class, I launched my own business in architectural interior design just one month out of school designing beachfront homes, restaurants and airplane hangars. I didn't know that the economy would take a crash just a year and a half later and force me to take on such small jobs as furnishing rental properties and eventually become a server to make ends meet. After working hard and doing everything right, I was nowhere near where I wanted to be and had become lost. I tried to remember the last time I had been truly happy, which happened to be on a college trip to Europe, where I had promised myself I would return the moment I graduated. Years later, I knew it might hold the answers to what I was looking for - I had so many skills, so many opportunities to achieve greatness (prescribed by others), but what did *I* want out of life?

It took a year of saving to take a solo three month sabbatical abroad, and it took nearly two months of that just to get the lifelong endorsed chatter in my head to quiet down. I had to dig deep to realize what it was that truly made me happy and with that sole mission on my incredible, sometimes terrifying and painful, but ultimately rewarding journey across Spain, Portugal and Morocco, I finally tapped into what painted that picture for me: being creative, living in the present, having the flexibility to travel, inspiring others, and having a family of my own one day. Many people I believe go their entire lives without taking a deeper look at what those simple key ingredients are for them; not what they've scripted for themselves, or what was perhaps the makeup of another person's recipe.

Seven years later, I now live in Hawaii with my husband (whom I met while working in the restaurant) and our identical twin girls, and I support our family creating original contemporary artwork inspired by my natural surroundings. Fortunately, many have found my work to be pleasing and my paintings reside in homes and businesses across the globe. To say that I am living the dream is an understatement. Could I have fast-tracked to this place of success right out of college? Without a doubt, no. Each job, each lesson, and each skill set I learned along the way helped shape me into the successful businesswoman I am today. But most importantly, the steadfast perseverance I held through it all to do the best I could in any given job, while never dismissing my bigger dreams.

In my father's moment of desperation, he got back on his bike with nothing but his determination, and he rode on a higher intuition that said it would all work out. It was on this life-altering journey that he realized the significance of forming relationships and aligning yourself with others that share your dream, and not letting yourself stop even when the obstacles are seemingly impossible. He did not quit until his front tire was in the Atlantic Ocean. These off-the-beaten-path roads through forests, fields, historic pioneer trails, and ridiculous mountain passes represented so much more than their mileage count. This expedition would extend far beyond ten states and 4,700 miles, presenting him with the ability to explore his true character, oversee immeasurable challenges, and arm himself with the tools that would carry and support him through the rest of his life. Every turn of the pedal brought him closer to the realization that if you persist, you will push forward, and if you can keep pushing forward, your goal will become that much closer. This perseverance became his motto in life and every goal he set out to accomplish, he knew that with hard work, little by little, he would get there.

Fast forward to today, he is the principal owner alongside his twin brother of VITEK Mortgage Company, the recognized leader in mortgage finance in the greater Sacramento area. They've outlasted most banks and mortgage companies over the course of thirty years. Now doing business in four states, they are dedicated to supporting the community and are making small strides towards ending homelessness.

Growing up it was not a dream, but rather a reality in my home that whatever you set your mind to could and would be achieved if you were willing to put in the work. My mother, a young teenager when she met my father, was so inspired by this man that she, too, adopted his incredibly positive outlooks as if they were her own. He encouraged her to believe in the power of setting goals, of positive affirmations, and of manifesting into reality the hopes and dreams they shared, far beyond what she had ever before considered possible. Together they were an incredible force and achieved more in their early twenties than most do in their entire lives. In first grade my gorgeous twenty-four-year-old mother would pick me up in her Porsche 911 Carrera, my father owned and piloted his own Cessna, and they had just finished building their custom dream home. Sadly, but amicably, their ten year marriage did not last forever and the tumultuous times that followed in the wake of their separation forced us all to face much more relatable circumstances over the next two decades. They both continued to affirm their ambition and work ethic to live a successful life and continued to the top of their fields, bizarrely friends through it all.

As I have continued to encounter roadblocks in my own life's pursuit of success and happiness, I always had the foundation I needed to help me reach my goals. Yes, my parents *told* me that I could do anything I wanted in life, but more importantly, they *showed* me. What greater gift is there than not only reaching your goals, but showing your children what they, too, are capable of?

The impact of your decisions not only fill the pages in the story of your life, but imprint their values and vision into future generations. At any given point, my father could have quit and no one would have questioned his reasoning, for after all, he was but a fifteen-year-old boy on a bicycle. But how different would his life have turned out? And how different would mine have turned out? Would I even be here today? My mom, who speaks of the handsome young man who wandered into her church one day in a flowing white tunic and spoke of rainbows and a kind of spirituality she had never encountered, would probably say no...

*Want to know more about this incredibly true story? Follow our journey as my father and I retrace this 4,000 mile passage through an updated visual narrative of photography, a new original art series, and the completion of my upcoming book ... coming 2018. www.anovaturientjourney.com*

## MEET PHILIP DUNCAN and LEANNA WOLFF...

**Philip Duncan** works with his twin brother Harry as the principal owners and leaders in residential lending at their company, VITEK Mortgage Group, in Sacramento, CA. Their company has been serving their communities for thirty years with nearly a billion dollars in loan servicing. As the company's first originator of home loans, Philip's vision and expertise in sales and marketing have been instrumental in establishing VITEK as an industry leader with brand recognition in the regions they serve. Today, Philip's focus is on providing exceptional marketing resources to their sales team, along with business development to support the company's growth initiatives, including builder, reverse mortgage, cultural and geographic diversity.

Prior to joining VITEK, Philip was a top producer of home loans for many years. \He began his lending career with Mason McDuffie/Weyerhaeuser, where he rose to Assistant Branch Manager. He then became co-owner at Criterion Mortgage Corporation before joining VITEK. In 2000, he was recognized as Sacramento Association of Realtors® Affiliate of the Year. Today he serves on the boards of the Sales and Marketing Council for the North State Builder Industry Association and the executive board of HomeAid, whose mission is to end homelessness in the Sacramento region through supporting with builder expertise and material and volunteer work to all the non-profits that help bring people back into the community, including Volunteers of America, WEAVE, and many more.

Philip graduated from the Mortgage Bankers Association School of Mortgage Banking and is a certified Toastmaster. He earned a BA from the University of California, Davis in International Relations/Political Economy and also attended one year at the Universidad Compultense in Madrid, Spain. He is fluent in Spanish.

Philip is a second-generation lender and native Sacramentan who is actively committed to his community outreach projects. He is known as an outdoor adventurer who enjoys white water rafting big rivers, skiing mountains, and scuba diving the world. More than anything, he believes happiness comes from having a mission greater than himself, and service to others is most important.

*Philip can be reached at* _pduncan@teamvitek.com_
*Website:* _www.teamvitek.com_

**Leanna Wolff** was born and raised in California. Developing an affinity for the arts at a very young age, she was quick to pick up anything that allowed her to use color and line to create and she won a few noteworthy awards for her skill beginning as young as age six. Continuing to develop her artistic abilities throughout school, she became affluent in numerous mediums including pastel, pen and ink, painting, sculpture, and writing. She received her formal training at the Art Institute in San Diego, graduating number one in her class in Interior Design with a strong emphasis on Architecture. While enjoying a successful career in design, she began expanding her artistic expressions to include graphic design, photography, and painting.

It wasn't until moving to Hawaii in late 2012 that her life took a sharp turn into the art world and her pieces have quickly sold from galleries across the islands. In just four years, her works now reside on walls in homes and offices across the globe and a dream has become a reality for this artist. Her passion comes from her desire to inspire people's everyday lives through the emotional experience they feel when viewing her art. Inspiration comes not only from working to achieve this goal, but even more so from these beautiful islands and the clarity it can bring to truly living in the moment.

Leanna's creative spirit, love of the outdoors and experience in architectural interior design has sustained her a niche to work with clients on private commissions, understanding their spaces as a whole and giving visuals that are unique to her process and skillset. The abstract waves expressed in her pieces are done with thoughtful and passionate use of color, emotive brushstrokes, and a flair for capturing movement. By incorporating crushed collected sea glass, sand, shells, washed up microplastics, and lava aggregate into her paints, there is truly a piece of Hawaii that goes with each original work of art.

Settled in Oahu with her twin girls and husband Otto Wolff, the family works together to create every piece, the two-year-old twins helping to collect beach glass, shells, and microplastics while Otto studies and documents the water through his photography and hand stretches every canvas. Bringing awareness to the current state of the ocean and how to rid it of the waste and plastics our lifestyles worldwide have contributed to its devastation is a passion that runs deep in this family. For every painting sold, Leanna donates $100 to Sustainable Coastlines Hawaii, helping to fund them in making a difference in our ecosystems.

### *Contact Information for Leann Wolff*

Direct:    (808) 551-0039

Email:     leanna@leannasart.com

Website:   www.leannasart.com

# WHEN PLAN A FAILS...
# IS YOUR PLAN B READY TO BE UNLEASHED?
### By Kathy Fairbanks

*"What you're looking for is already inside you."*
*~ Anne Lamott*

It was one of those effortless conversations with my boss, and I don't even remember how we landed on the topic of our mutual career plans in the first place. We both knew there was still much work to do in order to make a real difference in this world. During this fluid conversation, I realized that one item I had neglected to ask my boss when I joined the company just five months prior was how long he planned to remain the president of Klemmer Leadership Seminars, Inc., before he retired. Strategically, that was a big miss on my part, because neither of us were in the beginning of our careers. I was forty-nine and Brian Klemmer was fifty-nine.

His heartfelt and reassuring response was perfect as he convincingly talked through his plan to go full steam until sixty-five, then taper off and hand over the reins to the next generation of Kimberly Zinks and Scott Cundys of the company - the young pups, as he fondly referred to them. Then, at seventy, he planned to be in a position in which the day-to-day activities were undemanding of his time, which would allow complete focus on speaking engagements around the world. Brian thrived in front of an audience. He was the real deal, never over-produced, and he focused on showing up authentically every time.

Whew, Plan A worked for me! I knew I wanted to continue working until somewhere between sixty and sixty-five and then slow it down a bit. What I didn't know after a mere five months into selling for the training company was that Klemmer would never feel like a job. Instead, I would become passionate about introducing as many companies, individuals, and communities as possible to this very experiential training tethered to a Compassionate Samurai mindset.

What, you may ask, is a Compassionate Samurai? Brian coined the term as he authored his #1 bestselling Wall Street Business book entitled *The Compassionate Samurai, Being Extraordinary in an Ordinary World*. I've found it to be a worthy challenge to raise the bar in life by cultivating character traits that promote behaviors of a disciplined warrior yet ensuring that the traits of compassion are infused liberally as I navigate through all aspects of life. The result of a Compassionate Samurai mindset exhibits a balance of the best kind of leadership with magnetic development toward commitment, personal responsibility, contribution, focus, honesty, honor, trust, abundance, boldness, and knowledge. And yes, sometimes I succeed and sometimes I learn in this ongoing development.

So, in October of 2009, my Plan A was in place and I was learning how to promote the training programs as well as Brian from the stage. We travelled, connected with prospective corporate clients, and had a lot of fun. Every weekly meeting was a boundless lesson in wisdom and vision, not always easy, but certainly worth the journey. All was going just as planned - until it wasn't.

On April 7th, 2011, Brian Klemmer passed away unexpectedly, and the world lost a visionary leader and friend. For me, Brian's death was not one of a family member; it was the loss of a friend, a neighbor, a boss, a mentor, and a light. My heart hurt; it still does. I wanted to learn so much more from him. After his death, I craved more brain dumps. I missed observing him as a genius in action. But no matter how much I wished for Plan A to reappear, Plan B was creeping in like a steady unstoppable tank. I was on the tank ride, just not in the driver's seat of my own life at the time.

One thing that everyone who knew anything about Brian was that he had a 500-year plan – not a Plan A and Plan B, but just one 500-year plan. Who does that? Well, that's another story for another time, but it's important to know that the "why behind the why" of Brian's 500-year plan is the belief that we're much more than our bodies here on Earth and we certainly leave a wake with every action taken. I'd like to be able to tell you that I immediately jumped right into year one of 500 boldly and with focus. I didn't. Although it never dawned on me to quit and go back to my previous career in financial services, I was lost and waiting for someone from inside the company to fill Brian's shoes in my little corporate world of promoting Klemmer trainings. No one did, at first; it was not their passion or gifting. The facilitators are brilliant and truly world-class, yet corporate sales is not their calling. It's mine. I love selling. I see it as building clean relationships while connecting need to solution and very much centered around integrity as well as insuring that clients produce the results they say they want. Fortunately, my parents planted that mindset long ago with the trainings at Klemmer serving as the "cherry on top."

My leader recovery quotient was pretty low at the time of Brian's death and I continued to tell myself that I could never fill his shoes. That's true; however, after eighteen months, I got very intentional when I realized that I could actually fill a bigger pair of my own shoes. Ironically, I received a version of those wise coaching words from Kimberly Zink the day after Brian passed and she was giving of herself, trying to console me. She said she was choosing not to ask why but instead, to look at this as Brian's way of making room for everyone on the team to step up as much larger leaders and fill the space of growth. I knew what she was saying made sense, because, with Brian leading the way, I didn't have to think as big, be as creative, or undercover the hidden dominos. He was always there to do that.

Although it took me a couple of years to find my way and my voice, I did find it. I went back to school and studied the books, listened to the audios, and attended all of the trainings Klemmer offers as often as I could. Today, I'm blessed with another brilliant mentor in Kimberly Zink, the "young pup" Brian talked about back in 2009. She is now the President and CEO and leads as co-owner of the company, along with Brian's daughter, Krystal Zellmer, who is wise beyond her years.

So, what was stopping me, keeping me stuck, just "stirring the soup" but not dipping it up? Fear, resistance and the damaging mindset of "it just shouldn't be this way." As I grew more and more intentional about connecting corporations to the trainings Klemmer offered, I mentioned to Kimberly that I wasn't sure about the "how to's", but I knew that I was meant to promote this transformational work. I simply needed to get out of my own way and be the best of me. In many ways, my new mantra became the John Borroughs quote: "Leap, and the net will appear."

In late 2014, I became even more intentional about my mission. One of the foundational learning modules that Klemmer Leadership delivers around the world is a formula for success. We refer to this formula as the "Formula of Champions" because, once mastered, it's inevitable that champion moments will result. The formula is simple at first glance. In fact, although it's obvious and logical, it's necessary to drill down deeper, beyond the conscious level of thought. At that deeper level, it becomes a bit of a challenge to apply the formula consistently.

Here it is:

**INTENTION + MECHANISM = RESULT**

Viewing the word intention as determination, a plan of action, or a purpose, it becomes clear that intention is not simply what we want or the willpower necessary to achieve it. An intention must be deeply personal. Often, companies will hire Klemmer because they are frustrated. "We told our employees what to do in the form of quotas, but they are not reaching our goals." We must explain that you cannot create an intention for people simply by telling them what to do or how to do it. They may pursue the goal out of compliance and lack commitment, while their true intentions are to be comfortable, not look bad, not be rejected or not accomplish the goal. Asking someone to do something based upon someone else's intention is like asking someone to care about something that doesn't matter to that person. An intention must be generated from the inside out.

In our Personal Mastery seminars, people tell us it is their intention to be financially independent when it is not truly their intention to be financially independent. We know this because they are not taking risks. They want to be wealthy. They have a wish to be wealthy. That is different than their true intention.

Have you ever heard "The road to hell is paved with good intentions?" True intentions are much deeper, stronger, and more focused than wishes. You can tell people's true intentions by the results they achieve, because intentions and results are always one and the same.

Did you set a New Year's resolution? Did you break it? If so, this formula says that keeping the resolution was not your true intention. Your true intention was something else. Perhaps it was to be right about why you can't keep your New Year's resolutions. Perhaps it was to be comfortable without challenging yourself. In contrast, an honest intention is deeply housed in our subconscious belief systems. With intention come focus, certainty and commitment – the "I know that I know that I know" feeling.

Even though I knew clearly what my intention was, I was unclear about the best mechanisms to attain the result of the intention. A mechanism is simply the process, the technique, the how-to. Imagine you are on one side of a room, and you are challenged to cross the room one hundred times, using a different "mechanism" each time. Perhaps you walk across the room and crawl back. Then you swim across and hop back. The walking, swimming, crawling and hopping are all mechanisms. After four trips across, perhaps you draw a blank. Ninety-six more trips remain, yet you can't think of another way to cross the room! At that point, suppose I offer you a $100 bill if you come up with a new idea in fifteen seconds! An idea will come to you, seemingly, out of the blue. However, it is not out of the blue. A scientifically proven process has taken place. "When the intention is clear, the mechanism will appear." Under pressure to succeed, our subconscious mind responds with a new mechanism. If your true intention is to not look foolish, you may or may not make it across the room. If your true intention is to cross the room, you will come up with a new idea. Your true intention always finds a mechanism.

When John F. Kennedy declared that America was going to put a man on the moon by the end of the 1960s, most people thought it was impossible because the science to do so, the mechanism, did not exist. But Kennedy's intention created the science or mechanism.

Since I knew there were an infinite number of mechanisms available to meet any goal and that intention would lead to mechanism, I didn't worry about the mechanism and, instead, remained focused on the intention and shored up any conflicting intentions to my goals. Obstacles like staying comfortable, not taking risks, and being overly concerned of what others may think of me were no longer part of my mindset.

As for result, it's the effect, the outcome, the consequence. In the Klemmer trainings, a great deal of time is spent unpackaging this concept of intention equaling the results. We dissect the formula and put it all back together again as we provide the tools for implementing this formula in all aspects of life from work creativity to relationships to health to finances, spirituality and beyond.

What I realize now, as I reflect on the genesis of my PLAN B, is that the most important encouragement for you is not to delay. Create a true sense of urgency to develop your PLAN B long before it's needed. I've shared below five key areas of focus, which supported me during the ever-evolving process.

## PLAN B

**PRIORITIZE** – Take time to gather a full inventory of existing tools and talents available to you today. Stack rank what's going to make the biggest difference in your goals. Reverse-engineer every goal to insure the steps are in place for success. Assess what's working today, what's not and what's next. Then ask, does this priority list align with your purpose, your passion, your mission? If so, move on to leverage. If not, tear up the paper and regroup.

**LEVERAGE** – Reach out to community, your tribe, for support. Find and attract the best mentors for your goals and ensure the relationships are reciprocal– not equal, yet a two-way street. Are you of service and support to your mentors? Check in and assess who's supporting your growth, as well as who's working against your growth. Is it time to move folks in or out of your inner circle? Find an accountability partner or coach to increase the probability of attaining your goals. It's easy to be slippery alone, much more difficult when others are your cheerleaders. Make sure your coach or accountability partner is committed to having an open, honest and responsible form of communication with you.

Remember the "Emperor's New Clothes". Stay away from those missing a backbone. Remember that leverage and asking for support is a deeper level of vulnerability that can be quite an attractive character trait to master. I'm still working on this one.

**ACTION** – Stop waiting for someone else to take the lead. It's one thing to have a plan; it's another to actually take action. Sometimes, it looks like baby steps and sometimes it's clearly giant steps. The key is forward movement, course corrections and looking at what's next. Rinse and repeat.

**NO** – This tiny little word is a complete sentence. It's beyond important to set healthy boundaries around time, resources, and anything else that matters. Everyone knows this by now, yet I have found very few who have mastered the "art of saying no." One of my learning lessons from Kimberly Zink was to always ask the question...is this a win for our client, a win for the Klemmer team and a win for you? If the answer isn't a 3-way yes, then it's time to say no. Sometimes it can take a bit more of the Samurai in us than the Compassionate side, yet it will support us in producing the results we say we want.

**BEINGNESS** – This is the "get out of your head and into your heart" kind of stuff. This is the vulnerable you, the real you, the part of you that is willing to fall down, dust yourself off and try again. It's the authentic you without a mask, without make-up, designer clothes, lots of academic letters trailing your last name, VIP titles or a bank account rivaling Warren Buffet's. It's about becoming comfortable in your own skin and also becoming comfortable with being very uncomfortable. It's not "Can I do it," but "Will I do it?" Some of my inspiration around this concept came from Shonda Rhimes's book *Year of YES, How to Dance it Out, Stand in the Sun and Be Your Own Person*. Not only is it a great read, but also, as I read, I felt like I was hearing stories of inspiration and truth from a girlfriend. If it's been a while since you've been in this zone, tap into your muscle memory. If you've never been in the "Beingness" zone, start looking for evidence of your strengths, your gifts, and your talents. They're there, waiting to be discovered and shared with the world. I'm moved by the wise words of Eleanor Roosevelt, who said, "You gain strength, courage, and confidence by every experience in which you stop to look fear in the face." Be you, embrace you, thrive as you!

You may be curious about the specific nature of my intentional commitment set in 2015, and the results. My intention was to step up to become the "lead-off hitter" for Klemmer and work to ensure our trainings become a household name. It's a beautiful work in progress. Sometimes I really get a good chuckle on how irony shows up in the various forms of mechanisms in order to produce the results I say I want. The phrase "be careful what you wish for" rings true here. If I were to list (and I did) 100 different mechanisms to promote the training of Klemmer to the corporate world, I would have listed the following at the very bottom of the list as they **WERE** all way outside of my comfort zone. Yet each one served to promote our trainings to new opportunities and avenues, which never would have made it on my original wish list. Now that's the power of intention!

✓ (October 2015)          Walked in a Macy's fashion show for charity.

✓ (April 2015 - Current)  Write feature articles for *Wealthy Women's Magazine*

✓ (August 2016)           Conducted a video interview with radio personality Joel Roberts featuring our Klemmer training programs.

✓ (Oct. 2015 – Current)      Became weekly radio host on Voice America Talk Radio for "The Compassionate Samurai Business Hour"

✓ (April 2018)               Contributing author for *Breaking Barriers*

✓ (Summer 2018)              Future launch of my leadership book

Most importantly, while I was pulling out all the tools in my Klemmer treasure box, I beat uterine cancer. Beginning with my out-of-the-blue diagnosis in May of 2015, leading all the way through my surgery in July of 2015, my Plan B was invited to change. The recovery was humbling and I received incredible learning lessons from this speed bump of life and am so grateful for the grace provided by the team at Klemmer and Voice America.com, who embraced a refreshed version of my Plan B.

One of the best things I invested in as my intentions gained clarity was to find a business coach. He's brilliant and with his permission I've included some notes of empowerment by Coach John Dulworth from NYC:

Dear One –

Please be kind to yourself. When you find that you've not kept that promise you made, please be kind. When you forget or procrastinate or fall prey to laziness or choose for the umpteenth time, someone else's happiness at the expense of your own, please be kind.

Here's the deal...we all drift from our intentions...every single one of us. One minute we're riding high, connected to our beauty and strength, keeping those promises to ourselves and the next, we're upside down, dropping things, bruising the ones we love and forgetting everything we claimed was important to us.

Sweet pea, that's just how it works. This living – this life of yours – it's a practice and every practice includes drift. You will drift from your intentions. It's how you know they're important to you. The drift is what makes you more able to stick to them. As with any intention or practice, you plan for the times you lose your way. When you catch yourself as having drifted, pause, slap a smile on your face and return to your intention with gentle but firm loving compassion.

What you don't do is berate, or shame, or judge. Use the drift to make you stronger, more resilient, more understanding. Don't use it to become a better bully. We each stumble. That's a given. How you get back up. That's the key.

Smooches,

Your inner hero.

If your Plan A has passed you by, I challenge you to develop your own Plan B and unleash it now. I drifted for a while, but I found my way back to my highest level of intention. Take yourself on and step out of that proverbial comfort zone in order to play a much bigger game of life. Become a Compassionate Samurai in your home, your profession, in your cause, and in your community. Reflecting back now as meetings and conversations would come to a close with my mentor Brian Klemmer, I often heard him cheer, "Knock 'em Alive!" That's my intention for your success in breaking barriers: unleashing your Plan B and "Knocking 'em Alive!

## *MEET KATHY FAIRBANKS...*

Kathy Fairbanks is a Director of Client Solutions and leads the Klemmer Leadership Seminars corporate team, providing experiential training introductions to clients worldwide in order to support them in achieving their desired goals. She's honored to serve as the weekly host of "The Compassionate Samurai Business Hour" on Voice America Talk Radio where Kathy and guests share stories and tools for overcoming obstacles and creating shortcuts for sustainable results in business.

Prior to joining Klemmer, she enjoyed a dynamic twenty-year career in the financial services industry, focusing on new business development for CitiGroup and GE Capital where her boldest accomplishment was winning, losing and then winning again a $96M equipment finance deal. Connecting her strategic business skill sets with the 10 traits of The Compassionate Samurai insures a perfect match of deliverables from the Klemmer Leadership team in order to make a real difference in the way organizations operate and shift to a mindset of WIN-WIN. Campaigning for the Klemmer mission statement of *"creating bold, ethical leaders who are committed to a world that works for everyone with no one left out"* is always at the top of mind.

Prior to entering the financial services arena, Kathy attended Indiana University's Kelley School of Business and received a B.S. in transportation & public utilities management.

She is honored to serve on the Advisory Board at Pathways for Veterans in support of veterans and their families to create full and abundant lives, post military service.

Kathy and her husband of thirty years live in Marin County California and are the blessed parents of two young adults, who are both recent Klemmer Leadership graduates.

### Contact information for Kathy Fairbanks:

Phone:     (415) 250-4444

Email:      kathy@klemmer.com

# REINVENT, REBUILD, RECREATE, and RENEW: THE JOURNEY OF DECISIONS AFTER MY WORLD WAS IN RUINS
### By Cami Ferry

The mission of my chapter is to provide you, my dear reader, with a step-by-step process by which, if you find yourself in a "rut" or "slump" or something worse like a major crisis in life, you can bring yourself out of stagnation and begin to move steadily forward toward a rejuvenation of yourself and your life. That will eventually aid you in achieving the Breakthrough of the Barriers that hold you back from becoming the best version of yourself and living your purpose. I use my own journey in hopes of inspiring you to take these action steps and never look back and, more importantly, never, ever give up on yourself because YOU are WORTH IT!

Albert Einstein is accredited with having said, "Insanity is doing the same thing over and over again and expecting different results."

The first step in this process of moving toward the barriers that hold us back in order to break through them is to see, recognize, and accept our destructive patterns and habits that are not serving us in life, acknowledge our self-doubt and negative self-talk that feed our sense of worthlessness, and admit when our relationships and life situations are toxic and unhealthy. Only after we see and accept these chains in our lives can we begin to change our minds, hearts, and actions to achieve different results. Otherwise, we are stuck in the patterns of insanity.

Breaking these chains is often easier said than done. I personally spent twenty-five years in an emotionally abusive and toxic marriage because I refused to become what I considered a failure by having a broken family. I subjected myself and our six children to this toxic relationship because I was in denial of its destructive nature and I was completely committed to not losing the battle for unity of the family. This could be considered a noble characteristic, but when you look at the flip side of this coin, I was basically teaching my three sons and three daughters by example that it was okay and normal for a man to get drunk and treat his wife badly. I am ashamed to say that I did not leave even when it was very clear that there was no hope of reconciliation, when all was clearly lost.

Sometimes it takes a major catastrophic event to shake us up and wake us up to the facts that our own self-destructive patterns are the Chains holding us back. That is what had to happen in my life for me to see that I had to let go of what I thought should be the outcome and start to create a new vision for my life. In my case, it was my husband who, in a drunken fit of rage, finally took the abuse to a level of no return and then spent an entire year not speaking to me. The verbal battery was bad enough and should have brought me to my senses, but I had been through this with him so many times before that I figured it would play out much the way it had in the past following closely to the pattern of the cycle of abuse. It was the year of silence, intended by him to make me feel guilty and worthless, that gave me the time to contemplate and finally come to the decision to move on, to move forward into an unknown future.

The path of letting go is often wrought with much resistance and I can certainly say that this was the case for me. I grieved the loss of what I had held to so tightly. It was not so much love of my husband, as that had been destroyed many years before due to consistent neglect and abuse, but rather an ideal of what is right and what is true and good. I was clinging to my concept of what marriage and family should be and how staying together despite all odds was the true, good, and the right path, regardless of how bad things became. I lost myself in this battle as I had put aside so much of who I am. My self-esteem, self-worth, and self-love had all been destroyed through verbal and emotional abuse, but also from the negative self-talk that had become the mantra in my own head. At times I even became despondent and suicidal as I allowed fear to engulf my thoughts, but I didn't stop making decisions that changed my results. No matter how depressed I felt, no matter how bleak and frightening my future looked, I kept moving forward to break the chains of my own destructive patterns that had been so ingrained in my thought processes from years of verbal and emotional abuse.

I was determined to reinvent myself in the business world since I had been a stay-at-home mom and my WHY was to be able to financially support myself and my four youngest children so that we could live independently of my husband. I knew that I had to be away from him to break the chains of emotional manipulation. I was committed to rebuilding my future vision, which at that time was completely clouded in fear of the unknown, but still I continued to walk one step at a time into that future and, in doing so, my vision began to take shape as my life's passions began to awaken. Persistence is key to breaking through barriers and breaking the chains that bind us. Moving forward, even if only in "baby steps", is imperative to achieving those extraordinary results and outcomes in life that we all so desperately desire but also that we deserve.

In the wise words of up-and-coming music artist, Kenny Henry, from his song* "Breaking the Chains":

"You can break the chains today.

Listen to your spirit; it knows the way.

Say goodbye to the pain of yesterday.

It's time for you to stand up and break the chains."

If you find yourself in a less than desirable situation in life, whether that is an abusive toxic relationship or a dead-end job that leaves you feeling unfulfilled, or any number of ruts, slumps, setbacks, stalls, and depressions that can arise in life when we are not living up to our potential for greatness, when we are trapped by our own destructive beliefs and behavior patterns, then it is time for you to stand up and break the chains! See them for what they are, recognize them, become aware of them, and make the necessary decisions to change the patterns so you can achieve your breakthroughs.

The next step in this process is to realize and accept that you are not alone and that help is available to you. This, too, can often seem easier to say and even to think than it is to actually accept and utilize. For some of us, asking for help and guidance is one of the most difficult things to do. I know it was for me. But it is imperative to understand that we, as humans, are social creatures and we need to be connected with other humans in order to survive. The saying that "No man is an island" is absolutely true. Reaching out to others who have been through what you are going through and are where you want to be is like receiving a lifeline when you are cast at sea or a compass when you are lost in the desert. Seek out assistance whether that is from trusted friends and family, business networking, or organizations that specialize in personal development.

In my case, I leveraged all three of these lifelines in order to recreate a new vision for my life, one that was powered by my passions. I sought trusted friends and family to help me through the emotional valleys and depressions as I struggled to quell the negative self-deprecating voices in my mind and the fears fed by self-doubt. I sought business networks in order to connect with people who could guide me by example in how to maneuver the task of creating and building a business. I also made the decision, after being exposed to their model of training, to pursue courses in self-development and leadership through Klemmer and Associates, which is a Premier Leadership and Personal Development company. Through my work with K & A, I have become open to the opportunities and possibilities all around me and, thanks to their experiential model of training as well as the relationships that are built with others during the courses, I now have an arsenal of tools to rely on so I can continue to move forward making bold decisions and never settling for ordinary when I know I can achieve extraordinary results! I highly encourage you to check out Klemmer and Associates, attend a Champion's Workshop near you, or just go to their website, www.klemmer.com. But do make the decision to seek out assistance because you are not alone in this world and you deserve the support of others.

For me, learning that seeking help and accepting help does not devalue my journey nor rob me of my achievements but, in fact, enhances every aspect of each breakthrough, was an intricate part of the process. The magic in shared human existence and the bonds derived from it is what opens us up to the flow of the highest vibration energy, which is love. Assistance can come to you in surprising and unexpected ways. You simply have to decide to open yourself to the possibilities.

Finally, we are all faced with decisions every day and each decision brings us either closer to or further away from breaking through our own barriers. The key is to reevaluate as you go along the journey of each new day and be aware when those habits and patterns that hinder your progress start creeping into your life. Be willing to reinvent yourself when necessary if you discover that the path you are on isn't working for you or serving to draw you closer to where you want to be or who you want to become.

Rebuilding a new life from what seems like the ground up when all that you had worked so hard to build for so long seems to have been laid to waste and is in ruins isn't easy and does require commitment, focus, and even risk taking. There are and will be setbacks along the way, but persistence and leveraging assistance from others will keep you moving on the right track. In the end, only you can make the decision to recreate the life you dream of and deserve. Understanding your own self-worth and realizing that you are worthy and deserving of the greatness that you were created to achieve and the abundance that you were intended to live is so important for your progress toward breaking your own barriers and achieving extraordinary results in life.

Daily renewing your mind through consistently developing your character through books and courses, renewing your body through exercise and activity, and renewing your spirit through prayer, meditation, and deep breathing will help you to strengthen those three core areas of your being, which will in turn allow you to break through your barriers to become the best version of you - The Extraordinary YOU!

The song "Breaking Chains" is by Kenny Henry who an incredible singer & song writer. Please visit his website at http://www.KennyHenry.com to hear his music and learn more.

## *MEET CAMI FERRY*

Cami Ferry is the mother of six wonderful children, three boys/three girls, and grandma to her grandbabies, Nathan and Cassy. She was also very blessed to be the caregiver to her mom, who has positively influenced her life in many ways and was her biggest fan until her passing on Oct. 11, 2016.

Cami is an actress, singer, and dancer with thirty years of professional training and experience in classical theatre, opera and voice, as well as ballet, jazz, and contemporary dance in London, England and the U.S. She is currently pursuing training and partnership for professional and competitive Latin and Ballroom Dance. She has recently entered into training to compete and win in a Body Physique Competition. Through her company, In Motion Theatre Company, she has not only directed and performed in high quality professional stage productions, but has also co-produced, directed, and starred in award winning Independent films.

She is an international bestselling author, having written several articles for various publications and co-authored eight anthology books, including *Women On A Mission*, *From Fear to Freedom*, *Echoes in the Darkness*, *100 Voices of Inspiration*, *Awakening & Empowerment*, *WOM Sisterhood of Stories*, *3Ps to Success*, *Women of Faith*, and *The Beauty of Color Poetry* which have all been #1 International bestsellers. She is participating in other anthology books that are in the works including *Breaking Barriers, Chocolate & Diamonds for the Woman's Soul, The One Element*, and many others as well as planning a series of her own books which she hopes to start publishing by next year.

Cami is passionate about Creating, Becoming the Best Version of Herself, Loving, Respecting, & Valuing Each and Every Human Being, and Promoting, Empowering, Inspiring, and Positively Influencing the Hearts, Minds, and Lives of Everyone she encounters.

Founder/Artistic Director of In Motion Theatre Company, Founder of Cami's Cardio for which she is currently completing her certification as a Health and Fitness Coach, Radio Show Personality - The Theatre Queen, Founder and CTQ (Chief Theatre Queen) of The Theatre Queen Publications, Productions, and Media Broadcasting Company, a licensed financial professional - Life & Health Agent with Exertus Financial Partners, a Worthy, Focused, Abundant, and Prosperous Woman.

### *Contact Information for Cami Ferry:*

Direct Line: 209-663-9953

Email:          cferry@InMotionTheatre.org

Websites:   http://www.InMotionTheatre.org

https://www.facebook.com/cami.e.ferry

https://www.facebook.com/InMotionTheatreCompany/

# A GIFT TO STAY
## By Katherine Gerardi

Today, I am a Transformational Coach, public speaker, artist, and Emotional Alchemist. I was not always this way. I started out wanting with all my heart to be a pilot.

Flying high at seventeen was a great place to be, because down below, I had a father battling colon cancer, and he was not winning. The fearlessness I had to fly worked great on adventure, but very poorly on hospital visits. My courage crumbled at the threshold of any hospital my father was in and promptly turned into a deep desire to run.

So I ran...often. I had to drive to the beach once a day like medicine, just to see the waves. I felt like them. Each one building like courage, then, crash! There is something in the way that they never stop trying that inspires and comforts. My sanctuary was the ocean and sky. It was the greatest escape from the sad part of life ever.

Then one day, the tingles came.

I noticed one morning that my thumbs were tingly. My big toes were tingly, too. It was light and mild, so I dismissed it. If flying could minimize the awareness of a slow death by cancer in the family, surely a tingle was effortless to obliterate. It was. However, the next day, the tingle was a bit stronger, and it continued to worsen.

Soon, my feet were fully numb and my hands felt like tingle mittens. This did NOT stop me from flying. I cleverly wore shoes that were a bit too tight so I could feel the rudder pedals when I flew.

One morning, however, I ended up on the floor instead of up in the sky. Face first I went into the carpet at my apartment. Much to my surprise, I did not have the strength to pick myself up.

I called my mom, and she came to help. I staggered to the car with her to get to the hospital. As we exited the building, a bystander made a joke that I looked like I had been drinking. It was beyond awkward.

Meanwhile, my father was at home, fully supported by Hospice Angels. He was in the home stretch of preparing to cross over. Luckily, my father was a doctor who still knew many other savvy medical colleagues. An excellent diagnostician was able to come and take a look at me. I was declining. It was happening swiftly.

After a flurry of tests, a very sudden group decision was made to make a very heroic journey before the limits of my diagnosis kicked in. I did not know that what I had could kill me, potentially fast.

My family home was only a few blocks from the hospital. I got plunked into a wheelchair and pushed right to my house. A few helpful volunteers picked me up chair and all, up the front steps, into the house, and all the way up the stairs into my father's bedroom.

Somewhere in there, I had been told it was my last chance to say goodbye to my dad. I had been diagnosed with a very rare disease, a syndrome called, Guillain-Barre, and it is known to be potentially deadly. At that time, doctors knew very little about how to fight it. I knew even less.

I had been avoiding my father's room. Somehow, I think I hoped that if I did not visit, he could not die. Now here I was, barrier broken. I was in there. Looking at him. Oh, please, no. He looked so pale and thin.

I remember only fragments because I truly felt horrible, and so did he. Suddenly, we had the worst sort of common ground. It became the bridge between my denial and his reality. There was nowhere to run. There was no plane to fly, and this was a blessing - a big, huge blessing in disguise because it made me face it all before it was too late.

After a long silence, he pointed to my heart. "Kath, I am gonna be right THERE. And I am going to be telling you, 'Get off your back.' Please don't be so hard on yourself. Okay?"

I nodded, crying.

I don't remember that we actually said "Goodbye" before I was brought back to the hospital in a daze. His last sentence hung in the air like a big bell had been rung.

How could this be real? I was told later that my father had sworn an oath to live to see me through to my hospital discharge. It was ambitious because he had little time left, and potentially, I didn't have much time either. The disease was advancing.

The Guillain-Barre syndrome had started at my fingertips and my toes, and was headed to my body core to shut it down. As the nerve systems broke down, the functional control ceased, my body went more numb, and the weakness took over. In some cases, it can kill a person in an hour. In others, it can stop at the knee. Mine kept creeping in.

The staff knew my father, so a decision was made to keep me off a respirator so that I could talk to my dad on the phone. This was HUGE and profoundly ironic that it allowed my dying father to coach me to fight for my life.

When the disease clawed its way to my chest, my ability to draw a breath was suddenly ruined. Before long, I barely had the strength or control to summon enough breath to laugh or even to cry, let alone scream.

Over the coming weeks, I sank deeper. Eleven times they drained all my blood, separating the plasma from my whole blood and putting it back in with new plasma. It didn't change a thing. Each procedure took five hours. It was torture for nothing.

Through the whole ordeal, I had one book that was like a light in a very dark place. It was the book by Richard Bach, *Illusions*. I would ask for it to be read aloud when they were about to stick me with needles. I learned that if you pay attention to something awesome, it takes your mind off of the yucky. Remember that. It matters.

The quote that stuck with me the most from the book said, "There is never a problem without a Gift for you in its hands."

Really? In this mess? No way. No waaaaaaayyyyy. Except it stayed with me, and bothered me because it felt true, but I did not know how that could be possible to find a treasure in a horrible nightmare like this.

Finally, the "ultimatum day" came. The doctors had held off putting me on a respirator, but my breathing was getting too shallow. My body was drastically withered, and my spirit exhausted. I was given a midnight deadline to end my decline and level out, or I would be hooked up and unable to speak anymore.

There was a floating idea inside me that I should just leave with my father. Why not? We could go together! I was buried alive anyway, and paralyzed all over for what felt like forever. I had gone from having the freedom of the sky to the inability to breathe enough to cry.

Maybe the Gift was getting to leave?

Close to midnight, I felt myself drifting off into what felt like a big dark tunnel. Soon I felt very far away. I felt my spirit leaving my body. Then I heard a voice. It was yelling. It was angry! The voice said, "You do NOT HAVE PERMISSION TO DIE! I AM NOT DONE WITH YOU YET!" It was my best friend, and she was mad!

Her voice filled my ears. Something was different now.

I was different. I came back from the 'far away' I was.

Right then and there, the disease stopped progressing.

The tide was turned.

"There is never a problem without a Gift for you in its hand."

The respirator was dismissed. For the first time, I held my ground and stopped getting worse.

After the weeks of being on my back staring at the ceiling, I finally graduated to being sat up to see the TV on the wall for the first time. I was thrilled to watch a show and was really loving it, when I realized I needed to pee. So at the commercial, I got up and went to the bathroom.

It took me a moment of looking around at the interior of the bathroom, wide awake, before it hit me that there was no physical way that I could actually be there. I had just been allowed to sit up and did not have the ability to walk yet. There was no possible way that I could be where I was. Yet there I was having a real, O.B.E (Out Of Body Experience).

"So, if I go **here**, does it happen **there**?" I wondered to myself as I peeked around the bathroom door and saw my body back in the bed. Hmm... I was feeling that was a "Yes". I wished myself back in my bed with all my might, and POOF. I was back and pressing that nurse call button FAST!

"There is never a problem without a Gift for you in its hands."

My one quick Out of Body Experience was like a drink of water in the desert. I was so fully transformed by the raw excitement of how that experience rocked my whole awareness. If THAT is possible, what else IS possible?

The key was that thousands of times in my life before, I have gotten up to go to the bathroom during the commercial. It is a trained habit. Yet this time, I literally FORGOT that I was limited. I broke the belief barrier. Boom.

Soon after, I learned how to walk again for real. I got my discharge papers, and my Father crossed over twenty minutes later. I wasn't sad right away, I was happy he was free and out of pain.

He broke the barrier and left. I broke the barrier and stayed.

I never flew planes again, but I did go on to recover all my mobility and study martial arts, leadership, self-cultivation, and the vast expanse of what the human spirit can do to transform feelings that are rooted in fear or hopelessness into the treasure of choice.

"There is never a problem without a Gift for you in its hands"

I am now the living commitment to never take for granted a million different things after being buried alive in my own body. It was an experience that redefines the meaning of possessing freedom.

So many parts of this experience drove me far into the depth of my creativity of how to endure. It forever transformed my capacity to persevere. Now I teach others how to create the pivot points that access Possibility and the 'Gifts' that build the tide turn.

The most important virtue in success and survival is to persist. Therefore, the barrier that is vital to break down is any belief or despair that would make us give up.

I wanted to quit and die. The suffering was literally suffocating me. The Gift this problem had in its hands that broke me through to hope and recovery from the brink was made of many parts: my parents, my caregivers, my family and friends, a miracle, and a book written by someone I had never met.

This experience still fuels me to be a treasure hunter for the Gifts that can be found in any problem, and to ask ourselves lovingly, "What else IS possible? If THAT happened, what ELSE can I do when I forget I can't?"

When life feels like being buried alive, I invite you to look at any problem, and hear me whisper deep into your heart, "Don't give up. Look for the Gift, it IS HERE. I promise."

## *MEET KATHERINE GERARDI...*

Katherine is a Transformational Coach, Emotional Alchemist & Clarity Mastery Expert, Co-Founder and Executive Speaker of S4L Solutions4Life Health Care, Wealth Care and Self-Care.

Katherine has been called the "Secret Weapon" and "Queen of Clarity" for numerous coaches, therapists and professionals due to her meaningful systems that work, which put an end to further stoicism. She works with extremely powerful people who do not have time to be slowed down. Her work immediately clears the blocks to receiving: Success, Prosperity, Love, and New Opportunities that lead to momentum increase, sustained energy for high performance, powerhouse perseverance, and a deep inner knowing that "Everything is an Advantage NOW". She has been cherished at countless events, seminars and conventions, on stage and behind the scenes, creating flow and harmony so that others may shine when it matters most.

She is a grounding force of peace in the midst of chaos, and is also known for being "The One Conversation Transformation Expert" who has powerful "Same Day Results" tools for clearing emotional energy blocks, restoring momentum, converting fear into action and problem solving with Goddess/Oracle insight and Intuition fully engaged.

KATHERINE GERARDI
TRANSFORMATIONAL COACH

Katherine does ongoing private session work, group masterminds, workshops, and has a wealth of testimonials available upon request.

She draws upon over twenty years of leadership, teaching and volunteer work for non-profit organizations and success in the professional arena in addition to being a Martial Artist, Reiki Master, Spiritual Advisor, and Powerful Intuitive Guide.

# LET YOUR PAST INSPIRE YOUR FUTURE
## *By Chanra Hai*

"Dad trusts you, Dad loves you." Those were the last words from my father, who had passed away in December of 2007 and who spoke only limited English. A little over a month after that I had Jyzel along with postpartum depression. The memory replays so vividly this time of the year, every single year.

Jayda whispered to me, "Babe, I'm going to leave for work. Dad fell on the carpet. You should check him on him. I don't want to be late for work, and it's time for me to leave."

I jumped up from bed with no hesitation to check on my dad. I found him on the carpet in the living room, sitting there looking unstable and trying to hold himself up. So I asked him, "Are you okay? What happened?" He just slurred and I couldn't really understand what he was saying, but with the last few words he said he wanted to shower. He had obviously had a bowel movement on himself because the aroma filled the room.

I decided to pick him up and head towards the nearest bathroom. I removed his clothes. I turned on the hot water and let it run for a good five minutes but for some reason, it was still ice cold. As we waited and waited, he became anxious, so he grabbed the shower bowl and poured water on himself. After six cold times, he dropped the bowl, his eyes rolled back, and he completely passed out in the tub. I caught him in time. I never realized that my father was so heavy. His whole body weight was being pushed against both of my arms as I tried to hold him in a sitting position. I couldn't bear the weight, so I yelled for my mom. My uncle at the time was visiting from North Carolina so both he and my mom came. They helped me move my dad from the tub to the towel on the bathroom floor. I wiped all the water off of his hair and body then ran to his closet for the brand new sweat clothes I had bought him the day before. Mom grabbed the phone and dialed 911. I spoke with the dispatcher and they mentioned that they were sending people right away.

He finally woke up on the bathroom floor like nothing had happened. I asked him, "Are you okay? How are you feeling?"

The slur went away and he responded, "I'm okay. What am I doing here?"

I told him, "You'll be okay. We are going to carry you out."

So we all carried him out to his bed. Everyone massaged him and brought portable heaters close to him. He said he didn't remember what had happened.

The EMT personnel showed up. They came in asked questions about meds, his condition, took off his sweater, and checked his heart and blood pressure. I told them exactly what happened.

Fifteen minutes later they put him on the rollout bed and put a very thin white blanket on him. At this point he was wearing just his sweatpants, socks, and a thin blanket with no other top on. I asked, "It's extremely cold outside and it's foggy, can he wear his sweater?"

They said, "No."

So I asked them, "Can I go with my dad?"

They said, "Yes."

So I waited for them to put my dad in the ambulance and then I jumped onto the passenger side.

We waited for about another fifteen minutes with the back door to the ambulance wide open. I was completely covered with a hooded sweater and sweat pants and I was freezing, so I could only imagine that my dad was probably really freezing. All I remember while we were waiting was the laughter of all the EMT officials outside. I couldn't stand it anymore so I opened the passenger door and yelled out, "When are we leaving?"

One driver and two EMT personnel jumped in the back. They told me not to look back and I still until this day never understood why. Of course, I was stubborn and not feeling any better about the situation, so I turned back and looked.

One yelled, "If you keep looking back, we will not let you go with us."

I did not see exactly what they did to my dad, but after all of that, my father said that it was hard for him to breathe. "Dad can hardly breathe...Dad can hardly breathe." I cried and tried to convey to the EMTs that my father was having a hard time breathing. I'd never experienced anything like that. That was my third experience being in the ambulance with my father. They did not budge to even drive any faster. It felt like they were only going twenty-five miles per hour. Long story short, they finally hit the sirens right before they turned into the hospital.

They pushed my dad out from the ambulance and into the hospital room. The driver was telling me I couldn't be in the room with my dad, literally screaming in my face, "You can't go in there!" I told him that I was his daughter, his care provider, and his interpreter because he did not speak fluent English. The doctor finally told me I could stay.

I reached into my pockets looking for my phone, but I had left it at home. The only number I remembered was my house number so I called and called and called. Everything that could have gone wrong had gone wrong. The jack to my house phone broke. It took me multiple times to finally get someone to pick up and she hung up the phone. I tried again and again she hung up again. The last time I got through she yelled, "Stop calling my phone!" I was extremely frustrated at that point, trying to keep myself calm while one of the nurses was laughing the whole time while I was crying.

The doctor said, "Your dad is going to be fine." I calmed down.

They decided to hook him up to a respiratory machine and needed my signature so they could put him to sleep, so I signed it. I asked him, "Dad, do you trust me?"

He said, "Dad trust you, Dad loves you." He grabbed my hand tight and confidently went to sleep after the shot.

He was having a heart attack while he was asleep, so the nurse tried to shock him, but the equipment was not working. They did it by hand for a good forty minutes but there was still no progress, so they moved him to a different room. The machine in that room did not work either, so they brought him back to the same room he had been in before. I went out to call my house phone again, but no one picked up. When I returned to my dad's room, everyone had evacuated and left my dad by himself with tubes taped to his mouth. A nurse came to pronounce my father dead.

The female paramedic that had been in the ambulance came to me and said, "I'm sorry, if had known your dad was having a heart attack, I would have let them speed up."

I called my house again and again and again. My sister finally picked up and I just said, "Dad is dead. He is gone."

Two hours later, everyone started to show up, all of our family and friends. Then there was another strange event: a nurse from the pharmacy department came and gave me my dad's medication. I told her, "Thanks, but he does not need it anymore. He is dead."

The worst experience of my life is what drives me to seek for more knowledge. I wanted to understand the human anatomy, how the mind, body, and soul are connected, and how my father really died.

So I did my research and I came across massage therapy. I was never really the 9-5 type, so I thought, *This is me. I can help people, I can work out, work from home, be with the baby, and generate a good amount of income without anyone supporting me.* So I pursued it at Carrington College.

I found out during the last module of a massage therapy course that I was pregnant with Jyzabel, one month before I was going to graduate. I had to postpone my schooling until I had her.

On February 8, 2009, I gave birth a healthy baby girl, my daughter Jyzabel.

Two years passed after my father's death, and I still couldn't forgive myself for signing the document at the hospital for my dad to put him to sleep. Depression was still going on with postpartum depression.

My fiancé's mom passed also not too long after that. He also fell into a great depression. Now there was postpartum depression, loss of a loved one, and having to deal with a partner that became an first an alcoholic and then made the transition to illegal drugs.

I was a full-time mother at the time. He would accuse me of cheating on him and hear voices that were not there. His personality was the totally opposite of the one I had known for so long.

I was under lots of pressure. I was still committed to finishing my schooling for massage therapy, so I went back and finished it.

Struggling with all different types of depression, I one day decide to change my situation. With only $26.00 I grabbed my daughter Jyzabel and left the house. I told myself I would never put myself in that situation again. I went to my older sister's house and thought for three days about how I was going to solve my problems. And I did. I became homeless for two weeks with my babies to get away from the mental abuse from my children's dad.

I found a place in Bedlow that I could afford, a two-bedroom triplex that cost $600.00 a month. I made new friends with the neighbor Amy, her husband, and a handsome son.

I decided to go back to school for cosmetology and I did that for over nineteen months. When I graduated, I started my own business as a massage therapist, and I also worked at Wine and Roses. I loved my job. It was just a beautiful peaceful place to go to every day.

As a state certified massage therapist today, I understand exactly how my father passed away and I don't blame myself for it anymore. I am very passionate in all that I do and I plan to help others maintain their well-being and help people understand their bodies if they allow me to.

Prior to becoming a massage therapist I was an elder care provider for many years. I have older parents than most people my age. My dad, if he was still alive, would be eighty-nine years old. My mother is a well-respected elder in the Cambodian community. I came from a background of healers, musicians, farmers, artists, and community leaders. I love my children, my elders and my community. I learned so much from my grandfather, who would be 105 years old if he was still alive. He was an herbalist and a healer, My grandmother, who would be 106 if she was still alive, was a farmer and an amazing cosmetologist, My father was a classical music instructor from Cambodia, and my mother, who is sixty-nine years old, is a nun. Every single family member mentioned is known to do charity and community work in the Stockton Community and overseas. The first monk of the Stockton Temple off of Carpenter Road was my god father. He died at the age of 109 and that was many years ago. He renamed me prey-yeak-thusanak-thaivy. He mentioned to my grandparents and my parents that Chanra was not the right name for me.

I also worked at Dr. Ngac Tien Tran's office for almost five years as a medical interpreter and front desk receptionist, opening and closing the medical facility. From that job I met Cambodians form North, South, East, and West of Stockton. I've encountered many different stories from the Cambodian genocide to the happy times in their homeland, Cambodia. I thank Dr. Tran and his wife Mrs. Tran for taking me in and teaching me everything I needed to learn in a medical office.

Life was going great until April 2014, when I was rear-ended at a stoplight. That same night my neck felt like it was ripping off my shoulders and I had headaches and vomiting. I could not sleep. I slept at a friend's house because I was not able to drive and I did not want my mother to worry. My car was totaled.

It's been a wild roller coaster, and I'm slowly recovering from my accident, a back injury that caused sciatic pain. It hurts to sit, walk, and sleep. I am definitely not able to perform the duties needed for my work.

So I thought to myself, *What should I do now that I can't work?* Community work is something I've always wanted to do. I coincidently ran into a woman who had invited me to one of the Asian Chamber mixers. So I decided to go. I met Jim T. Chong, the MC of the evening, and I also met a chiropractor named Dr. Michael Arishan. I told Dr. Arishan about my accident case and he decided to take over my case. After several treatments, he had mentioned to me, "You probably won't be able to walk normally again."

I brainstormed for three days and decided to start my own business with the girls: Khmer Ballet of Stockton, since I wasn't able to afford their favorite piano lessons and gymnastic classes anymore. I thought about investing in the cultural influences with fashion, cosmetology, good food, and ballet. It would be something new for the community to get involved in. I wanted to work with businesses to help them prosper, work with temples and churches, and work with all organizations to bring entertainment and create confidence in our future American Samaritans.

This is where my journey begins, with my father's dream of a harmonized community for the Cambodian people to finally be happy all over again after over forty years of pain and suffering from which it is still in recovery. It is my commitment as a Cambodian American born here in the United States to carry on my culture, educate my children, heal my people, and impact lives in a prosperous and loving way. The Cambodian culture is one of the richest and artistic cultures in the world. We can definitely flourish with just a little Khmer influence.

Breaking through all the barriers was extremely hard mentally, physically, and emotionally. The most important thing to do is to remember to get back on track with a positive quote to start the day. I have to remember what my passion is and what my purpose is. Meditation helps to soothe the mind so ideas can be clearer. Getting a full body massage definitely helps with relaxation and removes tension from the body. Getting a scalp treatment for thirty minutes helps cleanse the scalp and also soothe the mind. Pedicures also helps soothe and relax the body. Healthy food with plenty of water helps also.

Remember to take care of yourself, but most importantly never forget where you came from. Let this be your guiding light so you can shine ever so brightly during your lifetime to perhaps light the way for others.

## MEET CHANRA HAI...

Chanra Hai is the founder of Khmer Ballet Of Stockton and also the Khmer Educational Endowment Network, which is focused on highlighting and preserving the Cambodian community. Through her story she conveys why she is so passionate about helping the people in her culture.

Chanra is extremely passionate and cause driven in whatever task she undertakes. She is also very focused on helping seniors and strives to someday help develop a Wellness center for seniors. Her background consists of working in the financial arena and uses her talents currently to help develop programs that accentuate the art and heritage. Her goal is to contribute significantly to connecting the Cambodian people with various opportunities to help them excel and also teach the youth about why the Khmer culture is so significant. She is establishing gateways of commerce to help give businesses opportunity to work with Cambodian businesses and to also help provide opportunity to the underserved people that have come from Cambodia.

### Contact information for Chanra Hai:

Email:       chanrahaiwellness@gmail.com.

# WHAT'S A DRUG KINGPIN GOT TO DO WITH IT?
## By Therese Johnson

My friend Cynthia asked me what it was like to be the wife of a drug kingpin. I wanted to burst out laughing, but just chuckled to myself. My ex-husband's illusions of grandeur had a far reach. He loved to embellish and tell stories of his days when he sold marijuana and smuggled 300 pounds at a time across the border from Mexico to California. I understood his habit of embellishing many stories, especially his drug smuggling days, but I got another glimpse of how much he had imprinted his narcissistic, self-determined magnificence upon our children and their friends. I could just hear him manipulating them by creating a kind of twisted hero worship of his image as a drug kingpin. I thought to myself, "Seriously?" Was that how he wanted his children to remember him? Was that how I was to be remembered, as the wife of a drug smuggler?

Shortly after I agreed to write a chapter for this book, I telephoned Cynthia to invite her and her husband to the Alzheimer's fundraiser event I was sponsoring. She told me she was going through divorce so I said, "I'm coming over." I offered my support and we bonded that evening and in the coming weeks grew our friendship.

I considered her a friend mainly because she had befriended my youngest daughter after my divorce followed by the aftermath from breaking up a family with six children. I was surprised that she had reached out to me, but over the next few weeks I supported her as she processed her divorce. Cynthia shared her impressions of me that came from conversations she had with my daughter over the years. She asked if she could see the photo of me in a fur coat, naked underneath and with money laid out all over a bed in front of me. I was amused at the stories Cynthia reiterated, all hearsay from my daughter since she was only two when my ex-husband was trafficking.

Apparently, her father had embellished this story as well. I had to disillusion Cynthia with the fact that the photo she was referring to did not exist and never did. I explained to her the story had been misconstrued and although there was a time I was wearing a fur coat, per her description, when my ex and I were in Boston, the photo of the money was taken in San Francisco on a different occasion with no fur coat involved.

Being a drug smuggler is not a romantic profession or one that I would wish my children or anyone else to be worthy of pursuing. It's bad enough to have to admit to having been connected to this man who viewed it as a profession worthy of pride or admiration. There was a romance between us, but it was not with drug smuggling. I had been raised a good Catholic girl by a father who was a Franciscan monk before he married my mother. Money and drugs were not something I considered of much value. I certainly didn't want the father of my children bragging about an illegal and dangerous activity. I was raised where we believed that sacrifice and hard work would get you to heaven.

When I first met my ex-husband, I was not tremendously impressed or attracted to him. He had been raised by capitalistic Jesuits and had a whole different take on Catholicism than what I had been raised to believe. We had known each other for about nine months and became friends while working at a restaurant when I decided to quit my job and move to Lake Tahoe for the summer. The month before I left for Tahoe, he surprised me by confessing his love for me. Our friendship changed after that and we started seeing each other over the long distance. I had never been in a relationship with someone of my own faith before so I found it refreshing.

He bragged about being a bishop's altar boy. I didn't learn about his drug smuggling for the first year and a half of our relationship because he knew I would definitely not want to be involved with him if he had told me.

He was very generous when we would go out with our coworkers. He told me he had money from a trust when I asked how he could afford to be so generous while supporting a family on a bartender's salary. We didn't date each other exclusively as he was still living off and on with the mother of his two young children. He convinced me that the relationship with her was over, but he was obligated to provide for her and his two young sons. It was only a relationship of convenience for his children's sake. I wanted nothing to do with him romantically as long as he was living with her and he assured me that he would not be living with her much longer. We continued our friendship and he continued to seriously pursue me romantically, though I was resistant and wanted to remain friends.

I enjoyed being wined and dined as he began courting me much more intensely. He did not like the fact that I had other suitors and he did his best to occupy as much of my free time as he could in between his clandestine lifestyle of drug smuggling (he would disappear for short periods of time), providing for his family, and working at the restaurant. He whisked me away to travel with him on short vacations so he could have me all to himself and to get me away from my other suitors. I began to fall in love with him and started to enjoy his lifestyle. I was a young, naïve girl in my 20s. I fantasized and romanticized about our "jet set" lifestyle, because we would take off to San Francisco, Boston, and Acapulco, Mexico at a moment's notice. By the end of the second year of our relationship, he was staying at my house with me and my seven-year-old daughter from my first marriage about 50% of the time and he had begun arranging child visitation and custody schedules with his children's mother. He wanted legal custody of his boys, which I thought was admirable at the time.

It was at this time that he began to reveal to me that he made some of his money by selling marijuana. He said he was just the middleman and sold pot only two or three times a year when a friend of his brought it from Mexico. I told him I wanted nothing to do with it and that I would never marry him (which he wanted) as long as he was selling marijuana. He continually assured me that it was only temporary and he would quit very soon and buy a legitimate business, within the year.

He moved in with me and I quit working, as he assured me we had enough to make it. I see now that he wanted me to be home so I could be at his beck and call. He did not want me to work where other men could steal me away from him since I would not marry him. I continued to attend university and passed up some opportunities to take positions with senators and an assemblyman. I was afraid to work for them because, although I was enjoying my fantasy love affair with this man and the lifestyle provided me, a drug dealing partner and my work in government would not have boded well, especially if my guy was busted for selling pot. Apparently and unfortunately, I did not value my own reputation in the same light at that time.

Being a single mom and a student, I was young and idealistic and thought I could change the world. I decided to go into healthcare and eventually I became an advocate for seniors. I'm proud to say that I did work at the Capital as a lobbyist and was instrumental in getting a Medicare reform law passed that created the assisted-living waiver project. This Medi-Cal reform allows seniors to have a choice in the type of long-term care they receive and is saving the state of California millions of dollars!

I desperately wanted to have more children. About this time I figured out that our Mexican vacations were actually work trips for him. I started to piece things together and began learning Spanish so I could understand what my mate and his friends in Mexico were talking about, since they rarely spoke English in my presence. He finally came clean about his actual involvement in the drug trade. He was actually a major trafficker, not just to friends, as he had previously indicated. When I look back on it now, I was gullible, naïve, and blinded by love. He put me on a pedestal and treated me like a queen. I had left my first husband after he physically abused me. It seemed I had traded in that scenario for a man who was a good provider, though by illegal and dangerous means. Understanding the scale of what he was doing presented a whole new moral and ethical dilemma for me.

It was the end of the 80s and everything was sex, drugs, and rock 'n' roll. Cocaine was the drug of choice for weekend socialites and university students like me. Neither my partner nor I actually smoked marijuana and we never liked the "high". We would drink alcohol and do cocaine socially when we partied on the weekends. We had bought into a local TV repair business, as he had convinced me that he was quitting smuggling and we now had a legitimate business so I could marry him. I desperately wanted another baby so I agreed to marry him, but not in the church, since he was still selling marijuana. He led me to believe he was now just a middleman. I had stopped partying and was focused on graduating from California State University Sacramento in 1988 with my Bachelor's degree in Government and getting pregnant. I accomplished both.

Originally, I went to college to become a lawyer. But when my mentor/ professor told me a Plato anecdote that the sign of a sick society was one with too many doctors and lawyers (unfortunately, I did not hear this till in my last semester), that is when I decided to go into a more nurturing profession and I ended up going back to college in 1999 to get a second degree in Gerontology.

I had wanted to open a care home for seniors for years and eventually planned to open one to support myself and my six children, thanks to a Filipino friend who had given me the idea to open one. But my ex-husband did not like my idea. I enjoyed seniors as I never really had any grandparents to speak of. My own grandmother on my mother's side passed away when I was a very young child and I don't recall seeing my grandfather except for maybe two or three times a year. We never knew anyone on my dad's side of the family because he was just three years old when his mother died and his father abandoned him at the age of five and left him to be raised in a boarding school. I felt I had missed out on having grandparents and maybe I thought somehow this might fill that hole.

I became pregnant three months after we married and had a boy. By the time my son was two years old, our five year courtship and honeymoon had come to an abrupt end and the true realities of life had begun to set in. My husband's weekends of drinking started to get closer together and included weekdays, and it became obvious that my husband was an alcoholic.

At my request, my husband went for a health physical and was told to quit drinking altogether or he would die of cirrhosis of the liver. So thus began his two year cycle of attending AA meetings and falling off the wagon, and my twelve years in Al-anon and recovery from co-dependency (with much thanks to John Bradshaw and his book *Healing the Shame that Binds You*).

In August 1987, we purchased a home. We needed a house that could accommodate the four of us and his two young sons, for whom he had gained custody. I considered his behavior childish and irresponsible, as he was just plain drunk all the time. I knew he was making bad choices because of his substance abuse and I feared a bust that would render him even less productive. Finally, he drove drunk with our son in the car and I left him for the nine months of his recovery work. Apparently, he never drank again. Confident in his recovery, we reunited and picked up where we had left off in creating our family. I had two more beautiful girls eighteen months apart.

Two events ended our marriage. The first was when he agreed with my decision not to invest our property's equity and went behind my back to invest the equity from our home anyways with a friend of his. He gave the equity to his friend to invest behind my back, without my agreement or approval. It was at that time that I no longer wanted to be married to him. The phrase "barefoot and pregnant" comes to mind when I think of this man's attitude towards me at the time. However, I did not think it would be in the best interest of our children for me to leave then, so I decided to just bide my time. This began what felt like my imprisonment.

Our TV repair shop partner had been repairing TVs and taking them out the back door to resell. The business went belly up, needless to say. I also suspected my husband had been lying to me about his smuggling. He said he had sold his smuggling business and was now only a middleman, helping to sell pot when they brought it back from Mexico. Out of the blue, he said he needed a vacation and was going to go to Mexico just as a "favor" to the guy who bought his smuggling operation. I begged, pleaded and cried, asking him not to go on this trip to Mexico. I had a very bad feeling about it and told him so. He went anyway, denying fear of imprisonment, like it would be an okay vacation. I had never felt so betrayed in all my life. This was the second event and was even worse than the financial betrayal of stealing my home equity without my consent.

The night the nine men from the FBI, DEA, and the sheriff's department raided our home is a story in itself and too long to go into here, but trust me, it was a very sad, frightening, and humiliating experience for my children and me. My husband was hiding out at a friend's house and spoke on the phone with the DEA agent while we were all being held at gunpoint. He refused to surrender despite the actions of the authorities. They had besieged our home, pointed guns at me, and ripped my baby from my arms while I was breastfeeding her to handcuff me. The agents advised him to get a lawyer and turn himself in to the jail, where he was fingerprinted and released to attend an arraignment.

While in prison for two years, he planned to get into shape and he left me with all the responsibilities of six kids with no job and $90,000 in debt. Furthermore, the $78,000 investment that his "friend" invested from our home equity failed. Our house was now mortgaged to the hilt and I had a newborn.

To be honest, I was relieved the marriage was finally over. I felt a huge surge of gratitude that my divorce was now imminent and would be attainable. I thought I would finally be free from this man, and the relief was overwhelming. At that time, I had no idea of the amount of guilt and shame I had been holding inside, or the mental and emotional abuse I had been enduring until that moment when, even in the presence of nine armed men surrounding me, I felt such a huge sense of freedom and joy well up and flood me like a warm blanket.

The ensuing years after that night were ones of lengthy grief, depression, embarrassment, humiliation, poverty, shame, and condemnation for me. Fortunately, I felt that God had been preparing me for this time and if it had not been for my faith, I do not know how I would have survived the years that followed. Strangely, I had more inner peace during this time than any other time in my life. Initially, I had to endure the public humiliation of my husband's photo and drug bust on the front page of the local newspaper. Then I had to face the parents and teachers of my children's Catholic school every day when I transported them to and from school, at church, and at all their school activities, sports, field trips, parent teacher conferences, etc.

I learned very quickly who were my true friends and true Christians and who were not. I was shunned by many at church and at my children's school. The worst part was that my children were also shunned. The pain and suffering I felt for inflicting this shame on my children was almost unbearable and I ached to run away and hide. I never cried so much in my life as I did for the six months after their father went to prison and I was left alone with all those mouths to feed. I had wanted to open a care home for seniors for years and eventually planned to open one to support myself and my six children. I was determined to provide a loving, caring, compassionate environment for seniors and my children and I knew I could do it, six kids and all! I eventually had to file bankruptcy to keep the creditors away, which only added more shame to my already full well.

Further shame came when the Knights of Columbus and Catholic men's organization (sworn to aid widows and children) asked my husband to resign after his public bust. Soon afterwards, a mother of one of the Boy Scouts in my son's den, which I had led, filed a formal complaint with the Boy Scouts of America. Because I hadn't been convicted of any crime and my husband was serving his time in prison and making restitution for his crime, they saw no reason why I should not continue to be the den leader. I am proud to say that five of my scouts went on to become either Life scouts or Eagle Scouts, my son included, and I stayed on as a Boy Scout leader serving the Boy Scouts of America leadership community for twelve years in positions of den leader, Boy Scout leader, committee chairperson, and summer camp trading post manager, among others.

Within months of my ex-husband's incarceration I did open a very successful State-licensed board and care home for seniors that I owned, operated and was the administrator of for six years supporting and raising all my children putting them all through private school with no help from their father.

It would take me years to recover from being shunned by my fellow parishioners and years before I even knew how that shame prevented me from letting my light shine. It kept me from sharing many of the gifts and graces God gave me. Boy Scouts supported me to be a leader and taught me leadership skills. I am forever grateful for my years of service to their organization and the opportunity they gave me to lead and to be a good role model for my son, and this helped restore my own self-esteem. This work also helped raise me out of my Catholic guilt and the legal, moral, and ethical dilemmas that haunted me for having been in love with a misguided man.

It was the kindness of my current husband that helped me to heal from all the years of abuse I had so naïvely accepted, unaware that if only I had been able to see my own value as a young woman, I may have made better choices. He helped me to see who I really was.

In 2016 with marijuana becoming legal in some states and here in California, the issue of marijuana has changed many people's perception of marijuana and pot smuggling. There seems to be less judgement about this kind of crime. Perhaps I would have had a very different experience today. Nevertheless, it wasn't until I shared this story with others that I was truly able to overcome many of the shameful feelings I had taken on from my husband's behavior. I found that others do not condemn me for being associated with a criminal or for being vulnerable to a loved one's manipulations and lies. In fact, I realized that I was much harder on myself than anyone else would be. My own perception of the shame as mine, when it was his, was condemning and debilitating.

I attended a seminar with Joel Roberts called "The Language of Impact." He is a famous Los Angeles radio host who was instrumental in helping me to reclaim my voice to share my expertise as a gerontologist on the radio. Additionally, I am a guest host on Jim Chong's radio show Rush Hour For Success on MONEY 1055FM with a segment called "Senior Moments." Joel Roberts encouraged me to express my shame during the seminar and as I did so, I was able to move forward and out of the darkness that had been keeping me small. Shame is insidious and creates more problems than we can imagine. Entering therapy also helped to debunk and dismantle the belief that I had done something wrong by loving someone who became increasingly controlling and disrespectful to me.

How many times have you felt yourself shrink or made yourself small enough to fit into some role? How many times have you kept your mouth shut when you wanted to speak out or given over your power to someone who didn't have your best interests at heart? Fear is a natural human trait and useful emotion when faced with danger. Fear can also make us choose what we believe will keep us safe, even when the opposite is true. It can make us believe that we can't do something, the cost is too high, we are wrong, the path ahead too difficult. Fear disguises itself with the voice of certainty, filling us with worry, doubt, and even dread. Fear is an emotion that can render us powerless and silent.

I wanted to pursue my dream of creating a nationwide Senior Service Directory and publish a book I have written called *Saving Seniors Savings: Best-*

*Kept Secrets on How to Pay for Senior Services.* I was terrified that someone would find out about my past connection to a drug smuggler.

"How could I be an authority on anything when I was carrying so much shame?" Everyone at the seminar assured me that I should pursue my dreams and not let the crimes of my ex-husband from over twenty years ago hold me back. In fact, I felt rather foolish that I had allowed myself to walk around with all that shame for so long, keeping me from pursuing other dreams and goals.

I am happy to share that as of September 2017 my book *Saving Seniors Savings: Best Kept Secrets on How to Pay for Senior Services*, was released on Amazon and became a bestseller in Elder Care and Aging and is available on Amazon now.

Sometimes, we need others to help change our minds about how bad or wrong we think we are. That is why it is so critical that we share ourselves and our experiences with others and why I am sharing my experience with you now. I can't tell you how many people came up to me at that seminar after I confessed the shameful secret from my past and told me how much my sharing helped them to give themselves permission to get past their own shameful experiences and forgive themselves. And when they started to share their shameful experiences, my own began to be so small in comparison that I was dumbfounded.

You don't need to stand up in front of a hundred people to dispel shame but finding a qualified therapist who can elicit those feelings will bring relief and newfound confidence.

If you feel your self-worth has been robbed in some especially shameful way, know that you can still pursue your dreams; you can begin to see your value and worthiness. You also can be an inspiration to your family and others. Sometimes talking about our wounds can free us from them. Once free, you can regain your self-esteem and power. It is critical for healing to be true to yourself, be honest about who you are, and live as you want others to treat you.

I would like to end with a wish for the reader from a quote from my favorite yoga teacher: I hope you aspire to inspire before you expire!

## MEET THERESE JOHNSON...

Therese Johnson is a gerontologist and an educator for the California State Legislature and the California Board of Registered Nurses (BRN). She is the author of the Best Selling Book **Saving Seniors Savings: Best Kept Secrets on How to Pay for Senior Services**. She also co-authored several other books and writes for international magazines, newspapers her blog as well as being a local TV producer, Radio show guest host for "Senior Moments" on 105.5 FM (KSAC) and iHeart radio and others.

Therese is the founder of Senior Care of Sacramento, a placement and resource referral agency for seniors. She is an Alzheimer's specialist and certified nurse's assistant. Therese is passionate about optimizing the quality of life for senior citizens, through taking an integrative medicine approach to their care, as well as engaging in social and financial advocacy on their behalf. Therese has spent the last 20 years working in acute care, long-term care and as an administrator for residential care facilities for the elderly.

While serving as the president and legislative advocate of Foothill Association of Care Providers for the Elderly (FACES), Therese co-sponsored and successfully passed the Medi-Cal reform law in California "Assisted Living Waiver Pilot Project (ALWP)", requiring Medi-Cal to fund RCFES and Board and Care – small, home-like environments offering seniors personalized attention, private quarters and dignified lifestyles. Prior to the passage of this bill, California Medi-Cal only funded skilled nursing facilities.

For more information about Saving Seniors'
**Savings:** visit http://www.SavingSeniorsSavings.com

*Contact Information for Therese Johnson:*

Telephone:   916-877-6904

Website:       http://www.SeniorCareOfSacramento.com.

Email:           caregiving@seniorcareofsacramento.com

Book offer at Amazon:

https://www.amazon.com/dp/B075HK7RQD

# FEARLESS
## By Mel Martin

It's Sunday afternoon. I ran the first half of the California International Marathon today. I'm beat. Actually, I did better than I thought I would do. I didn't expect to run this event, but my teammate and I decided at the last minute to get signed up for it. I had a high calf strain from a flag football game on Thanksgiving Day and I only had ten days to heal before the event. It's one of the things that I had to overcome in the last couple of weeks full of challenges. I'm currently building four different businesses that are merging together and earlier in the week I had a bit of a breakdown...a great cry.

As a professional coach, I certainly am not without expertise in other areas, so I have coaches that help me balance that out. I placed a call to one of my online super coaches and in this call, I told her that I did not want to discuss anything about improving my online coaching business, but just to talk about life. As I began to tell her everything that was on my shoulders, I just let it go and really started to cry. After that emotional conversation I felt so much better. Sometimes it's good to do that.

One of the businesses that I run is a HIIT group exercise club location. I coach twelve classes per week starting at 5 a.m. so I'm up by 3:45 a.m.. I've been doing this for the last four months and it has caught up to me. The rest of the day I'm running my other three businesses, an onsite and online coaching company and a distributorship in a nutrition supplement company.

I would have to say what got me through this this week is my ability to have overcome the emotional trauma that I endured literally from childhood. That emotional trauma along with a few other key events in my life have caused me to have anxiety. I did not realize that I had anxiety until about a year ago. I actually thought I was going through depression when in fact I was not. I learned that I also catastrophize. That is where you think of everything that you're involved in at the worst way and the worst outcomes play over and over in your mind. It can be paralyzing and very draining.

The cause of my anxiety began literally shortly after birth. My mom had rejected me because she felt she could not take on another child, so she gave me up for adoption. That was my first taste of rejection and abandonment.

My adoptive father was a soldier. He served in Vietnam and Korea in the U.S. Air Force. He used to beat me. He used to whip me with a belt and slap me across the face all the time. It was not until I was in my 40s that I reflected back on how he used to treat my mom and me and I realize that he had suffered from PTSD. He had all the signs: emotionless, closed off from the world, separating us from both sides of the family and making us live far away from everybody, rarely letting us be social with friends and family and just being intense and angry all the time. In truth, I lived in fear of him.

To this day, I am still not sure what had prompted this, but when I was eight years old, my adoptive mom decided she had enough of me for some reason and took me back to return me to the woman who had brokered the adoption arrangement. I remember crying and pleading to her to not leave me there. She ended up taking me back home, but the damage has been done. That was a major experience of abandonment and rejection. It would clearly affect me later in life.

My adopted parents and I had a falling out over a high school dance that I was invited to. My mom would not let me go and I guess I'd had enough and I flipped out on her. When I got home, my dad stormed into my room and proceeded to beat me to the ground. That led to all of my belongings being boxed up and packed and I found myself out the door at fifteen.

It was a very difficult period in my life, going through my high school years without the guidance, love, and leadership from a mom and dad. I lived with a new friend and his family that I met in a new high school. He was kind enough to take me in, but the next four years were very stressful. I always felt like an outsider, even though they did their best to make me feel like part of the family. It was probably because there were times when I felt like more like a housekeeper than I did a son. I'm grateful to them for taking me in and sheltering me and to this day, we consider each other extended family.

The next two decades were awkward and painful. A girl I was in love with broke up with me in my early 20s and I was devastated. I had no idea how to cope with it and it cost me my job because I couldn't handle it emotionally.

I felt a lot of anger towards my father. I remember feeling enraged and wanting to just physically beat him and even kill him just at the mere sight of the freeway exit sign to his house. This anger and resentment went on for a few years. It carried into a relationship I had in my early 30s. I ended up seeking counseling and it helped. The counselor took a chronological look at my life and it showed literally a lifetime of trauma.

The relationship I was in at the time ended painfully. I came home after work one night and caught her with another man. That event led to some serious self-doubt and trust issues for me. Luckily, years later, this former girlfriend and I talked about it and reconciled. We both understood that we were not fulfilling each other's needs and she admitted to me that she had made a mistake and apologized. I forgave her as part of my healing process and we ended up being friends now as more mature adults. All is well.

I got married towards my late 30s and spent fourteen years in a very anxiety-filled marriage. My former wife was brought up as a rather toxic and judgmental person. I created two personas: one man who left home to go to work and was himself, and the other who came home and shut everything down within himself to be the happy, smiling husband as he walked in the door. I had to always be pleasant and if I was anything less or vented about my day, she perceived it as me taking it out on her when in fact, I was just seeking refuge in our own home, which should've been my sanctuary.

We lost our fitness training studio franchise in 2008 due to a straining market and poor decisions I made as I desperately tried to hang onto our business. . Bankruptcies occurred after that and the pain from that led to our marriage being irreparable and subsequently ending in 2012.

Five years later, we both realize that we are better now as friends than as a married couple. We have a relationship now as co-parents to our awesome young teenage sons.

I've had one serious relationship since then that just ended this past March. I spent eighteen months with somebody that I fell deeply in love with and lost myself in the relationship. It ended up being a very hurtful relationship. I simply was not the man I should've been for her. She was definitely not the right one for me. Yet, we forced it. We tried to make it work and we never should have.

I was so weak in the relationship that I had to compromise my core values. She humiliated me in front of her children, emasculated me in front of her friends and family, and I allowed it.

The relationship ended badly. I learned a tremendous amount and I just tell myself that God wanted me to endure that so that the lessons would be hammered home into my head forever.

"I will never ever let that happen to me again."

"I will never compromise my values ever again for anybody."

Call me hardheaded, but it took all these events for me to learn everything that I know now.

I attended a major online coaching seminar in New York this past October and some of the activities we did really stirred my soul. I was really feeling a lot of emotions and intensity from it. So much so that I felt the urge to write and this came out of me during the flight home:

**G.I.V.E.**

**G: GIVE ALL YOU'VE GOT IN ALL THAT YOU DO!**

What you do at every moment echoes eternally so don't do anything half-assed. Do it right, especially when you know how to! MAKE THE BASIC SPECTACULAR SO THAT WHEN YOU NEED TO BE SPECTACULAR, IT'S BASIC. Because if you don't, you'll end up having to clean up whatever you half-assed, right?!?!

**I: INVEST IN YOURSELF; YOU'RE WORTH IT!**

Reinvent yourself. Refine yourself. Read a book and learn something new! Don't like to read? Then get an audio book app on your phone. HIRE A COACH. I'm sure you're pretty bright, but you're not that smart. You know what you know, no matter how educated or intelligent you are, but if you think about it, YOU REALLY DON'T KNOW SQUAT.

Here is the thing about coaching; A good program may cost a few dollars, but YOU'LL LEARN MORE. Don't be cheap. Spend the money. How high or low your return on investment is totally determinant upon what you give, so if you're gonna have an expert make you accountable, you might as well partner with a winner who'll MAKE YOU A TOTALLY AWESOME WINNER.

### V:   VICTORY AWAITS YOU. GO FOR IT!

Okay, stop with the weak excuses, stop listening to the lies in your head, and get out of your own way! Take a HUGE LEAP OF FAITH and GO FOR IT! IT'S INCREDIBLY SELFISH NOT TO! Holding back and failing to show the world your best can deny the world of a life-changing event, system, or something that can simply IMPROVE THE QUALITY OF EVERYONE'S LIVES! How do you think all the greatest things that have ever been invented are part of your life? People were passionate about it, believed in themselves, didn't care about what anyone said about them, took a risk, and WON - for all of us! So go for it because you'll win, and even WHEN YOU LOSE, YOU LEARN and that's STILL A WIN!!!

### E:   EMBRACE YOUR FLAWESOMENESS.

You've been shattered at some points in your life. You have been wounded and damaged and part of you is broken. If you believe that you're not, YOU'RE LYING, so stop it. YOU'RE UNBELIEVABLY IMPERFECT, but you're still here because you're a STUBBORN PERSON WHO REFUSED TO DIE, right?

Okay, so the bottom line is this...maybe you've been criticized and you believe the garbage and doubted yourself. Yes, people will talk trash about you. SO WHAT? Above and beyond the fact that it's probably not true, it's NONE OF YOUR BUSINESS what PEOPLE THINK or SAY ABOUT YOU! Actually, it's good that they are talking about you because that means YOU ARE RELEVANT RIGHT NOW. That kind of marketing is PRICELESS. Not caring about anybody's opinion of you is not only liberating, it allows and propels you to TAKE RISKS FEARLESSLY! The mere fact that YOU ARE THE ONLY ONE that exists makes you a totally ORIGINAL and AUTHENTIC SUPERSTAR. You are an accumulation of your broken pieces, all the painful experiences that you stubbornly overcame and refused to die from, your quirks and awesome unique talents. Those FLAWS, that FLAWESOMENESS, makes you TOTALLY AWESOME and don't you EVER let anyone tell you otherwise.

It's now very early on Christmas Eve and I'm on my way to take my dog to the groomers. I've been reflecting a lot since Thanksgiving. It has been a tremendous year. I've gone through some challenges, won some amazing victories, learned some very valuable lessons that I now apply every day. I live an incredible life. I can't help but just be grateful for everything in it. I have two amazing sons Ian 17, and Jacob 15. We spend a lot of time working out and laughing together, just what men do. They are also amazing human beings. Both are very kindhearted, intelligent, and athletic. They are my biggest why, my biggest inspiration to win every day! They are growing up so fast and I feel like I don't have much time before they go on to live their own lives. I work now with a purpose every day to gain freedom so that I can do the things I want to do with them and not be tied down with having to trade hours for dollars to survive.

That purpose inspired me to write the M.A.R.A. Method:

**M: MOMENTUM**

Stop procrastinating! TAKE MASSIVE ACTION NOW and CREATE MOMENTUM and SET THINGS IN MOTION. You can easily have PARALYSIS BY ANALYSIS from over-thinking things. DON'T THINK...DO! On the days you don't feel like doing it, get off your ass and do it! Always be moving forward. TRUST THE

PROCESS. There always is one when it comes to succeeding in something and if there isn't, CREATE ONE! GET MOVING and FUEL YOUR MIND, BODY, and SOUL!!!

## A: ACHIEVE

MAKE IT HAPPEN! Don't sit around. Take all that momentum and ACHIEVE TO FEEL SMALL WINS EVERYDAY and GET CLOSER TO YOUR GOALS ALL THE TIME! Success is just a bunch of small steps you took to get whatever it is you want, right? There is also no right or wrong. Stop being fearful of doing things wrong. Self-judgment is the worst paralyzer of all! Trust yourself; you'll have plenty of time to go back to improve. If art is the risk and the relentless process of refining it, canvas after canvas or mold after mold until it's right, then treat your pursuits the same way. BE RELENTLESS and HAVE NO FEAR. Don't get in your own way. JUST GET IT DONE.

## R: REFLECT

PUMP THE BRAKES. Sometimes you're so deep in the woods that you forget to TAKE A BIRD'S EYE VIEW. Soar really high above like an eagle to SLOW THE GAME DOWN so you can see all the pieces of the puzzle and all the players in the game. Reflect clearly to see where you can MAKE CHANGES OR ADJUSTMENTS so you can keep moving forward. YOU ARE WHAT YOU TOLERATE, so have the courage to eliminate anything that is not mutually beneficial for you. This is good practice for improving your decision-making skills because even after your trusted sources, you may have to ASK YOURSELF HARD QUESTIONS that require you to TRUST YOUR INTUITION TO ANSWER. Make sure you do the foundations and routines that make you successful every day. Feeling stressed is a perfect time to reflect because there's always something you're not doing that's causing it. FAILING TO REFLECT IS CARELESS and CAN COST YOU AT THE END so take the time to do it.

### A:   ADVANCE

KEEP MOVING FORWARD. Take all of MOMENTUM, ACHIEVE and REFLECT and KEEP GOING. Even WHEN YOU FALL, you always have to KEEP ADVANCING. You can break up the year in four quarters as your macro-cycle and each week as your micro-cycle and apply M.A.R.A. to CHECK YOUR PROGRESS and to KEEP YOU ON TRACK. It will help you BUILD CONFIDENCE IN THE DIRECTION OF YOUR GOALS and it allows you to SEE THE ACCUMULATION OF YOUR ACTIONS. We tend to FORGET THAT when WE FEEL DOUBT and INSECURITY in our lives. Just remember, THERE ARE NO RIGHTS OR WRONGS, only the OPEN-MINDEDNESS TO LEARN and MAKE ADJUSTMENTS. There is also NO SUCCESS WITHOUT A WHY because WITHOUT IT, YOU WILL ABSOLUTELY FAIL.

As you can see, G.I.V.E. and M.A.R.A. are tools to remind you of your purpose and to keep yourself accountable. All those years of emotional trauma, anxiety, and catastrophizing have led to these two powerful things that I live by.

I feel very fortunate to be thriving in my life beyond surviving and if you feel anything like what I described, I hope that what I've written can help you in some way.

I absolutely love coaching and inspiring others. I cannot think of a life where I'm not bringing the best out of others. If you need my help, I will be there for you. Whether it's to lose weight, gain strength and muscle, or just to help you think and feel better, I'm here for you and so are G.I.V.E. and M.A.R.A.

### MEET MEL MARTIN...

Mel Martin is a speaker, author and a health and fitness expert. For over thirty years he has had the fortune of empowering and elevating a diverse array of clients from post-cancer patients, law enforcement and military, to major-league baseball players. His more recent title is Over 40's Wellness Specialist and Men's Empowerment Coach.

Mel says that after he turned fifty he realized that his experiences in life were relevant to the development and empowerment of others. His online coaching company is FitLuvStrong: Effective Wellness For The Over 40's Who Want Lasting Results. His programs keenly focus on the human needs of people who have crossed the fortify-something threshold. At that stage of life, he believes that there's more to health fitness then just health and fitness. When asked about his own state of wellness he says, "At 53 I am in the best shape of my life because I practice and believe that you are what you do and you are what you tolerate."

His coaching style is authentic, empowering and real. Mel is also a lead coach for The Powerful Man, a U.K. based International Men's Coaching Group. Mel is also an empowered father who teaches his sons the lessons of life they need to know to be powerful men themselves. Through a series of Facebook livestream videos, Mel has established a huge following of people, empowering a virtual audience to live their best life now. No matter what season of life someone is in, Mel feels that loving within, being confident, taking action and staying fit and strong are critical keys to success.

### *Contact Information for Mel Martin:*

Direct:            (916)529-9164
Facebook DM:  http://m.me/mel.martin.169
Email:            mel@fitluvstrong.com

# MATTERS OF THE HEART
## By Marthella McWilson

As I sit and think about my life, I consider things that I have been through, the things that have brought me to my knees in pain, tears, and prayer...I also have to think about the things that have brought me pure joy and happiness. A flood of emotions, questions, and self-examination come upon me when I do this. I'm thinking about the times in my life when the decisions I made could either make or break me...when giving up WAS NOT an option. When tragedies in my life hit me...what is my reaction to it? What do I do next? Do I lay down and give up or do I get up and fight?

I was born in Joliet, Illinois not far from Chicago. It's a cold and windy city in so many ways like the environment and behavior of some of the people. My father lived there until his life was taken...a true LOSS for me!

I remember sitting at his funeral as a little girl. I was in the 6th grade and was playing with my cousin's hair. My aunt would always braid their hair and put beads and glitter in them which being in California it's just not something I saw before.

As they read the obituary I heard my name mentioned so it grabbed my attention. It made me start looking in the program with my Daddy's picture on the front searching for where my name was and also where my brother's name was mentioned.

Looking back at that time, I was sad, but the true feeling of loss came much later as I got older and could SEE AND FEEL the voids in my life not having him near me. The distance between us was one thing, but I knew I would see him in the summertime or family reunion and could call him if I wanted to talk with him.

Don't get me wrong, I knew my father loved me. The time we spent I cherished and learned a lot from him.

However, with the distance between Illinois and California, there was definitely a lack of the day to day presence of him in my life with many missed events and milestones in my life as a child. As I became a young lady and started dating, it became more evident that the lack of him in my life, no matter how wonderful my mother was, there was always moments I felt a hole, a missing but very significant piece of the puzzle in my life.

I wished he was there and that we could've spent more time together! You know, the times when you go on a date and when a dad would give your date a bad time. Unfortunately, that was not the case for me on a very specific date. I was taken advantage of that day by a man that I said yes to the date and I never would have thought he would not respect my NO later that day. My first time not by choice...It CHANGED ME RIGHT THEN!

Growing up I was a very outgoing person loving people, music, and life. I use to write poetry and songs, sing and dance, watch and play sports. Those were things that I USE to love to do along with being ever so inquisitive.

But being violated changed me to the core. I BLAMED MYSELF! "What did **I** do to make him feel that this was ok?" "God why me?" "What will people say...I mean I did go out on the date with him. Maybe I gave him mixed messages without knowing it? Was it my fault???"

After all the internal questions, most being unanswered, I became silent and closed off; however, not intentionally but that's just how I coped with it. Yes, I learned how to go through the motions and look like everything was ok when it truly wasn't. It became a way and standard for my life and how I decided to mask what had happened.

Looking back now, I would tell anyone that how I handled it was not the right way to deal with it. I learned that it's best to talk, tell someone that you believe will give you the support that you need to get through it. If you don't express and deal with it, you will hold it in your heart and be okay for a little while, but it will somehow come out in your behavior and not always in the best way.

For me I became silent, closed off, angry and not trusting of people...especially men. It kept me from opening up and letting people get close to me or my heart.

I prayed daily to God to heal my heart from the pain and loss I had up to that point with my father not being there. It was an intense anger with the feeling of being abandoned, used and abused. But worst of all, blaming myself for the rape. It was a real process to let go and keep going.

My mother was a great woman and my best friend. I could talk to her about any and everything. She always had great advice. My mother was diagnosed with Stage 4 cancer and was told she had 6 months to live. Fortunately, God on the other hand, said otherwise. I am so thankful that I had been given a little more time with her. I walked with her on her journey...**dodging landmines**, considering what natural remedies to consider, dealing with chemo appointments, and constantly searching different ways to heal. It was rough! I became a distributor of natural health remedies and gave to my mom that every day as we prayed for healing and for her to be comforted and comfortable as possible. God gave me another year with my mom since the diagnosis. She passed away in January 2007 when God decided to take her home.

I miss her so much! There is not a day that passes that I don't think about her, the advice she gave me, and the life examples she lived out in front of me daily. My mom truly loved God and she did everything she could possibly do to train me and my sisters up to be the best we could be both physically and spiritually. Mom taught us to believe in God, making sure that we knew that we had to nurture and create a personal relationship with Him so that we could give him praise and worship without faking it. Out of everything I learned, this was the best lesson she had ever taught me.

In me, I have created that personal relationship with whom I call my Father / Daddy, spending time talking to him and giving him my praise and worship whether or not I feel like it or when times are rough and doubt would try and sit on my shoulder to weigh me down and ask me, "Why do you believe? Look what has happened and is happening to you? What kind of God is that? Who do you think you are?" My faith answers the questions for me.

As a little girl, I had big faith. I believed what I was taught and no one could sway me from it. I pay attention to the signs given to me by God, I have deep conversations with Dad. He always tells me what to do, where to go, and what to say. However, like children I don't listen all the time and sometimes go off and do my own thing. The results don't end up the way I thought and I experience the consequences as we all do. As I get older and wiser thought, I definitely still make mistakes and fall but PRAISE GOD I have it in me to get back up

One of my nicknames people gave to me when I was young was "Ms. Nonchalant" probably because my behavior may have come across as being indifferent or uninterested. Which is another way I used to protect myself. But in "protecting of my heart" I also closed it off from anything good to come in but since then God also helped me learn to open my heart.

And then there was love. I was young and fell in love. No one could tell me anything. I had made some bad choices in dating early on. I had fell to my knees in prayer, broke down in tears, fought through anger and fear. I was willing to make the decision to open myself up again, trying to not bring in my feelings of mistrust into this new relationship. He was just what I needed at that time in my life as he was caring and a communicator. We talked for hours about everything. He was book and street smart, sensitive to my feelings, and very supportive emotionally and financially.

Life happens and situations came up that I could not move pass and forgive, so we were unable to move forward together as we had planned. We would break up but because of the strong connection and the soul tie that was created between us, we went back and forth in our relationship.

I became a teen mother at seventeen years old and needed to make the difficult choice that many are faced with...do I keep the baby? I made the right decision which was to be a mom! The gift in all of this is that the choice was one that truly changed my life for the better—not because it was easy, but because it was hard, which made me a better person as a result.

The fear of the unknown and then the self-talk and questions I would ask myself:

"How am I going to do this?"

"I'll be only seventeen when I have her."

"I have to finish school."

"I don't have a job."

I had to deal with the feeling that I would disappoint my mother which turned out to be to the contrary as she received me with open arms. Even so above all, I knew that I was not going to put this burden on my mother. I remembered an old saying "You laid in the bed now you have to make it." Truly my thinking was Now I Have to Make It Happen!

In writing this chapter, I've had to look inside myself and think about some painful memories that I had buried deep down inside me. But to be able to keep moving despite the challenges are also the same things that have created the test and trials that were designed for me to face and conquer to become the woman I am! I am so thankful that I can remember as a little girl the things I was taught in church, at home with mom, and all the times with my Dad both always saying the same thing, "Trust in God", "Baby girl, you can be whatever you want to be. What is it that you want to do? Nothing and no one can stop you but you. Be you. I love you."

Learning to trust in God and have faith that He would bring me through life as He did many times in the past, I hold on to the fact that I don't know everything but the one thing I do know and believe in the deepest core of my soul is that He did not bring me this far to leave me. I thank God that no one ever told me that trying to walk with God and do the right thing was going to be easy. No! I was taught that the people that love God will suffer persecution, go through struggle, pain and be tested but as the Bible states, "Blessed *are* they which are persecuted for righteousness' sake: for theirs is the kingdom of heaven." Mathew 5:10

Although taking an honest look at my life, many of the struggles and pain have been self-inflicted by myself due to some bad choices I had made through my emotion and what I wanted rather than what was right. Here is my advice about making decisions based solely on what you want...don't do it!

I am amazed at some of the decisions I had made that did not serve me well and thank God for forgiving me and saving me from the life that could have easily been forced on me by the consequences of my choices.

The power of choice is something a lot of people take for granted. I am fortunate to know many people from all walks of life environment and economic backgrounds: poor to very rich. gang members, drug dealers, strippers, pimps and killers in prison, business owners, doctors, police, lawyers, pastors and mayors. In talking with them all it's always something that happen that pushed them to the far right or far left. I am always intrigued to hear what it was.

I often say that I can learn from anyone, even a bum. People tend to look at me strange when I say that. I am truly sincere when I share that because I know everyone has a story and I am just one of many that you are able to read about now.

I would like to leave you with this thought:

If you don't know God personally, it's simple. Just say, "Lord Jesus forgive me." Then, just speak to Him from your heart as you would talk to your father, friend, doctor, or lawyer because he is all that! Ask for knowledge and wisdom daily in all things. It's a process. Don't give up and don't quit but rather FIGHT!

If you are looking for purpose, try looking at the **fruit of the Spirit** which is "love, joy, peace, patience, kindness, goodness, faithfulness, gentleness and self-control." - Galatians 5:22-23 (AMP)

Remember where you came from but also what lies ahead. Learn from your past to live your future! Remember the age-old statement:

*"It's not about what's on the outside but what's in your heart that matters."*

## *MEET MARTHELLA McWILSON...*

Marthella McWilson is first and foremost a great woman of faith. Her heart for God is demonstrated in her confidence that despite the life situations in her upbringing, she has dedicated her life to helping people. Her calm demeanor and matter of fact approach to life is one that sets people at ease when they are around her.

Having been in real estate for 21 years, she has embodied the ability to cater and adapt to the needs of her clients whether it be in developing a plan to acquire a home or securing the home of their dreams.

Marthella began in the Real Estate industry in 1997 as a loan processor working her way up to Sr. Loan Officer. In 2000, she started a loan department within an existing established real estate and development company. While managing and training her team in 2004, she obtained her real estate sales license and added listing and selling homes to my resume.

Marthella has a daughter and son, both of whom are approaching 30 years of age, and she serves as a Nana to a 5-year-old boy. She is also the foster mother/guardian of a brother and sister who are 13 and 18 years old.

Marthella has been an exemplary champion in overcoming many obstacles in life and has been a stable force and foundation to many that are around her including her daughter Shavet Alexander. Marthella's passion had also passed on to her daughter as demonstrated by Shavet's recently formed non-profit called Homeless Hearts, Inc. to help the less fortunate.

Marthella is also on the verge of opening a non-profit that will help establish a resource and transitional center that would provide counseling and financial literacy services to women that are in need of assistance in getting established in life. Through her life, she is looking forward to directly impacting thousands of women in crisis and to give them faith that they don't need to compromise but can live a life that God intended for them to have.

### *Contact Information for Marthella McWilson:*

Direct Line:  (209)430-7330
Email:  Marthella209@yahoo.com
Website:  www.RealEstateByMarthella.com

# FIRE - HELP!
# THE POWER OF A TEAM
### By Lindsey-Lan Nguyen

My name is Linh-Lan Nguyen and I am an eight-year-old Vietnamese girl who fled my motherland with my family in search for freedom. It was immediately after the Lunar New Year of 1987 when my parents took my four younger sisters and me to Cambodia to start a new life in a foreign land.

Every morning, I start my day by going to the market with my eight-month-old sister on my right hip and my three-year-old sister holding onto my left hand while keeping my eyes on my five and seven-year-old sisters to make sure they do not get lost. We sit down at the local food vendors for a bowl of congee or rice noodle soup before I call out, "Ma chan phrum hia", which means five Cambodian riels (៛; 5) per bowl of soup. (2016 exchange rate: $1 USD = ៛; 4,082.0 KHR).

The food vendor replies, "Phrum hia?" just to confirm that I was ordering the ៛; 5 bowl instead of the ៛; 7 bowl for the larger size.

My job is to make sure that my sisters are fed before I eat my portion, then we head on to buy fresh groceries for the family meals. I carry home a woven straw tote of fresh meat, fish, and vegetables to start cooking lunch for twelve people, which is comprised of my family of seven and the carpenters who work with my father, Minh, and his brothers.

One hot summer day, my family decided to go to a neighbor's house to relax after many months of hard work building boats and making paddles and furniture for local residents. I decided to cook a pot of soup on the brick stove that we built and fueled with wood chips from my father's boat shop. As I stoke the burning stove, I am unaware that the burning wood chips are pushed back towards the wall, which is constructed of the dried palm tree leaves. The 44° Celsius (120° Fahrenheit) intense dry heat made the walls of our stilt house as flammable as tinder.

When the fire broke out, I panic, but was afraid to use the good water from the tub to put the fire out. I grab the brass basin of water that is used to wash the vegetables and throw it on the fire, but it is unable to contain it because the flames are too ravaging. I grab a pitcher to dip into the tub of drinking water and frantically try in vain to put the fire out by myself. All of a sudden, I hear a man screaming in a foreign language.

"Phleung! Phleung!" That's the Cambodian word for fire.

"Fire, fire, help, there's a fire!" Mr. Hon is speaking in his native Cambodian language, calling out for help, when he sees my family's kitchen in flames.

Mr. Hon is our next door neighbor. When he saw the blazing fire, he starts to yell for help and my eyes light up with gladness when I see him. In quiet desperation, I begin to yell in Vietnamese, "Help, my house is on fire, help me, please!"

When my family hears the frantic screams from afar, everyone runs back home to find their house in flames. The men quickly take whatever can hold water and run to the nearby delta to scoop up water and together they put the fire out.

Fresh drinking water is scarce in Kampot Province, Cambodia because it is located by the inlet of the ocean.

Every family has a tub that stores drinking water, which is refilled by the waterman who pushes a pushcart throughout the village to sell to the villagers. The only source of drinking water is from the springs located in the heart of the Khmer Rouge territory and commoners are forbidden to go near those areas. If people speak up, they will reap the consequences immediately.

A coffee shop owner and his whole family were murdered by the Khmer Rouge Klan near our house just because he complained that the waterman comes too late in the day and that they didn't have enough fresh water to make coffee for their customers.

In order to save our drinking water, we often go to the nearby rice paddies, which are infested with leeches, to bring home fresh water for emergency usage. Some distance away from the village is the nearest well where we must travel daily to fetch fresh water for bathing and washing clothes. We use the shoulder yoke to carry two buckets of water home for washing dishes, vegetables, or personal hygiene.

Trembling with fear, I am in tears for burning the kitchen area and am so sure that my father would give me a spanking or that my uncles would scold me. Awaiting my punishment, I try to clean up the mess from the aftermath of the fire and the pot of soup that was cooking. Begging for forgiveness, I kneel before my parents, murmuring, "Mom and Dad, I'm really sorry about the fire. I didn't mean to burn the kitchen, but when I saw the blaze, I didn't know what to do. =I was too afraid to yell for help until Mr. Hon came over to rescue me. I will never burn the house again."

To my amazement, instead of punishing me, my father pulls me close to him by my shoulders and says, "I know it was an accident, Daughter. We're glad that you're all right. Just remember, if anything wrong ever happens to you, you need to scream for help. We were lucky that Mr. Hon saw the fire. If it wasn't for him, I don't know what would happen. We can always rebuild the kitchen. After all, we're carpenters. It's you that I'm concerned about. What would happen if he didn't call for help?"

I let out a sigh of relief upon hearing my father's words of wisdom and nod in acknowledgement. "Yes, Dad, I will remember. Thank you, Daddy."

"Phoektuk, phoektuk!" yells the waterman in Cambodian, which means, "drinking water, drinking water". As he pushes his cart by my house, everyone quickly calls out, "Phoektuk, phoektuk."

Two years prior, my father had left Vietnam to search for freedom because he kept hearing voices in his head that the Communists were after him since he went to Bible college and did not serve in the Vietnam war. On his first trip to Cambodia, my father discovered an easy way to escape to Thailand, but he decided not to go alone, so he went back to Vietnam to persuade two of his brothers to come along. Both of his brothers, Hai and Lam, agreed to join him to escape for a better future. They worked hard in Cambodia to earn enough money for the fare to Thailand. However, their boat was caught by the authorities and they were arrested for escaping the country. For a month in prison, the three men were sent to the jungle daily to chop down trees and were released shortly due to their good behavior.

Since all of their money had been used to pay for their failed voyage, my father and his brothers had no more money to return home to Vietnam. They set out to find work, heading towards the province of Kampot in the village of Peng Pau. There they met a Vietnamese family who were building their house. When the man of the house, Dan, saw the three young men looking for work, he asked if they were interested in helping him with the construction of his house. He promised to give them room and board and a little extra money. My father and uncle Hai accepted the offer, but uncle Lam decided to return to Phnom Penh and work for the ship building company.

After uncle Hai and my father finished with helping Dan build the house for his family, they decided that since there was enough land to build a boat shop, they would build boats to sell to the local fishermen.

A year went by with no word from my father and uncles. We didn't know what had happened to them. Finally, my father saved enough money to pay for his fare home to Vietnam, so he left Cambodia to reunite with his family right before the Lunar New Year. Not knowing that it was going to be our last New Year celebration before our lives would forever be changed, my sisters and I dressed in the most beautiful clothes to visit our relatives and wish them good luck and fortune for the New Year. We were taken away from our extended family, friends, and all the things that were familiar to us.

And that is how my journey as a foreigner began...

At first, I didn't quite understand why we were traveling so far on so many modes of transportation. We started out on a mini bus to Southern Vietnam and spend a night in a run-down inn. The next morning, we caught another bus to take us to the ferry then transfer to a little paddle boat, where the lady sailed us across the border of Vietnam to Cambodia.

My sisters and I were taught not to question authorities while we were growing up. We should be obedient children and just have faith that the people in charge know what they are doing. Just as the book of Proverbs 22:6 teaches, "Train up a child in the way he should go, and when he is old, he will not depart from it."

Until this day, I can vividly remember many lessons that my father taught me throughout the years, even though he is a man of few words. His actions speak louder than words can say. The biggest lesson that I've learned from my father is that in order to do something big, you need teamwork, because you cannot do it alone. In order to accomplish this mission, we need to surround ourselves with the right people.

For us to doing great things, we need to all pull together, just as everyone did when they need to put out the fire that I started in the kitchen of our house. My father demonstrated teamwork the way he operated the boat shop with all the carpenters so that when the fire broke out, everyone knew that they needed to pitch in to help save the house. They didn't need to be told what to do. Everyone just automatically grabbed something that could carry water to extinguish the fire and prevented it from spreading.

A key characteristic that I also learned from my father is that being kind can help a person build a better team. It's in our human nature that we sometimes would do things for others more than we would do it for ourselves. I have seen it over and over again, and when our family needs help, someone is there to help us in time of need. The key is that we need to ask for help, just as my father taught me. Many times, we are afraid to ask because we think that we can do it on our own. Our ego thinks that asking for help would show that we are weak, but oftentimes when we allow others to help us, they find it rewarding for them as well because they are able to make a difference in other people's lives. Mr. Hon was able to create a movement when he started yelling for help and everyone came together to put the fire out. I hope that my story will start a movement for you to create change in your life and your community.

### Lessons:

- How can we take opportunities of people around us to help us in time of need?

- How can we learn about other people to come and help them in their time of need?

- How can I start a movement to create change in my community?

*"Alone we can do so little; together we can do so much."*
**_Helen Keller_**

## MEET LINH-LAN (Lindsey) NGUYEN...

**Linh-Lan Nguyen** is an entrepreneur in the financial services industry, CEO/founder of Athena Wealth and Insurance Services, and an Executive Vice President and trainer with Exertus Financial Partners (EFP) who loves to empower people to become financially independent. Training is her passion where she speaks from the heart of her 15 years of experience in the fields and in the office. She has the charisma to take any audience from laughing to crying resulting in attendees taking action for lasting results. Lindsey facilitates workshops and seminars which encourages people to claim their financial freedom because she believes in educating people with the knowledge to navigate themselves to achieve their financial dreams and goals.

The oldest of five children, Lindsey was born in Vietnam and raised in Cambodia, Thailand, the Philippines, then immigrated to the United States of America when she was ten years old. Lindsey has experienced many hardships in life with near death experiences, but never lost hope that she has a greater purpose that God has in store for her. She has always been a role model for her four younger sisters and exemplify in her leadership abilities to those around her.

In her soon-to-be released autobiography, Lindsey will tell her life story in a candid way of all the miracles that happens in her life and how she has been breaking barriers to become the person she is today that will inspire you to overcome any obstacles in your life and change the world to make it a better place.

Lindsey is a graduate of Central Washington University with a bachelor's degree in Business Administration. Lindsey enjoys the outdoors such as beaches, picnics, camps, and road trips. She also loves to read, write, cook, scrapbooking, golf, and tennis. Lindsey is actively involving with San Jose Community Church where she is the playwright for the church's drama ministry and overseeing the college and young adults group.

### *Contact Information for Linh-Lan (Lindsey) Nguyen:*

Email:          LindseyLanNguyen@gmail.com

Websites:       www.athenawealthsolutions.com,

                www.exertusfinancialpartners.com

Facebook:       www.facebook.com/lindseynguyen22,

Linked In:      www.linkedin.com/in/lindseynguyen

# BREAKING THROUGH BARRIERS TO LIVING LIFE BIG
### By Nikki Nguyen

When I was a little girl I always wanted to do something big and meaningful, and I believe we all started out that way. We were taught to dream, write goals, and do whatever we want in life, but living that out is another thing. If you ever struggle on making the right choices to accomplish the dreams or visions that are instilled in your heart, this chapter was written especially for you!

I was raised in a family with five girls and me being the youngest girl, I got all the hand-me-downs from my sister. But I was okay with it. My family was on food stamps and neither of my parents could speak English. I would constantly see my dad come home drunk, arguing with my mom about money. When I saw that constantly, I couldn't wait to work so I could provide for myself and buy everything I wanted. My oldest sister had to be the parent in my life and to my siblings. I believe this incident in my life motivated me to work hard to be a provider not only for myself, but others as well. My family setback was a set-up to be an example for me to persevere through struggles.

When my parents first immigrated to America in Texas, they both had factory jobs. I was born in Amarillo, Texas and had to learn the American culture environment from school and friends. When I came home, I had to adapt to the Vietnamese culture that my parents never departed from. I saw both of my parents work very hard and do everything they could to provide for the family. My dad worked at Caterpillar repairing machinery equipment. One day he was in the hospital because his body got third degree burns from a work accident. He would share with me those times that he had to sacrifice a lot for the family. It made me see through the struggle of my parents coming to America and the price they had to pay to get here. They left everything they had for an opportunity of hope for a better future for their children.

I am humbled by my past, but I see it as a tool to inspire me to take advantage of every opportunity that I have here in America. I don't ever want to take it for granted. I learned that what is taken for granted can be taken away. I graduated high school and went to California State University. During those times I had a part time job scanning documents because scanners were very advanced back then. The company I worked for would scan court documents onto a disc to save storage, then we would shred those confidential files. I was getting paid by hour and it was about $4.25 back then. I was working part time and it was enough to get me by since I was going to college full time. Then I came across an opportunity to work at Cache Creek Casino. That job totally wrecked my mindset of not wanting to work for hours anymore. My one day of work at the casino was equal to a week's pay at my scanning job! So I was making great income working part time as I finished school.

When I graduated, a friend invited me to get license to be a real estate agent. Because of her I am in the position I am currently in. I now do personal investment and help others acquire wealth through real estate. This career opportunity helped generate a large source of income and gave me the ability to give back and fund different community projects and organizations.

I was raised a Catholic and was saved as Christian in 2006, which changed the trajectory of my life. My life was turned inside out and the void that I was missing all those years of soul searching, the missing link, was and is always God. I am proud to say that Jesus is my Lord and savior, yet I am far from perfect. My struggle in life became more real, but my Spirit became stronger. I always wanted to do something big in my life and one day, God made it became a reality. I knew in my heart he had called me to Vietnam, even though I was born in the state of Texas. I always felt in my Spirit that God has called me to serve in Vietnam. I would pray and feel the tug in my spirit and doors started opening.

One of my friends, Sharon, is a pastor's daughter and she always wanted to go to Vietnam for vacation/mission. So I took on the opportunity to go with her, knowing in my heart that God wanted me there although I didn't know why. Two of my other friends Billy and Heidi, went as well. The four of us headed to Vietnam for a mission trip, not knowing the agenda at all and praying for God to lead. When we got there, we were connected with a Korean pastor who was serving in Vietnam. He shared a powerful testimonial that he always wanted to go into business, but everything he did failed. He knew God had called him in to the ministry but he was being obedient. Then one day, when all else failed, he kneeled on the floor and he raised his hand. He said, "I surrender, Lord." The Korean pastor connected us to a Vietnamese pastor in the area and they had a lot of connections. I finally knew the reason I was there: to connect and bridge the American churches to Vietnamese churches and to support missionaries. I saw the vision to invite spiritual leaders from other nations and to equip the people of Vietnam. I left Vietnam with a mission.

When I came back to the States, I shared the vision that God had put in my heart to certain friends. Then I got connected with different pastors and big preachers. I attended a healing meeting. Dr. Gabriel Heymans was the preacher for the evening, and that is one of my best memories. I have never experienced God in such a way as in those late night meetings. I have been touched and encountered the power of the Holy Spirit. Then the vision kept coming back and I shared the vision with the preacher, and he is my spiritual mentor today. I shared with him that I felt that God wanted us to teach the Vietnamese leaders and equip them to know the Holy Spirit. They agreed and prayed on it, and then the planning started.

**BREAKING BARRIERS**                                    **Page 140**

We had two leaders that were going to teach and had been serving the Lord for years, Dr. Gabriel and David. We had the team of six or seven people going with us prepare for Vietnam. We bought our tickets and visas were made. Vietnam was preparing for 100 leaders in the South of Vietnam and 100 leaders in the North of Vietnam. Things were moving along as planned - or so I thought.

I came to find out that David was going through some financial issues with his family. He was a loan officer and during those times, things had shifted in the market and his income shifted as well. He is a father of six children and the main provider for the family for years. Finances were a huge issue in his life during that time and he had manipulated his title to getting people to do things for him for financial purposes because the financial weight was heavy. He was a controlling person who demanded respect because of his title instead of earning it. God was exposing the sin eventually. Dr. Gabriel saw that conflict right away and immediately knew that he couldn't join the platform and ministry with David, even though everything was already set to go. Looking back, it was a blessing that we didn't go. Even though everything was prepared it didn't mean we had to go. Dr. Gabriel was obedient to only one person and that was Christ.

My heart was saddened because I felt the vision that God put in my heart was his will. I didn't understand. I thought this was being done all for him. Why would He allow this to happen? Then I started to question myself. I started to doubt that I was hearing correctly from the Lord. I thought that was what He wanted. But why did it fail? I didn't understand. But we couldn't do a mission trip to equip leaders if there was no speaker or teacher.

Fast forward two years. I attended a mission trip in Brazil with Global Awakening. This trip was definitely a different perspective and tons of learning about healing and God's power.

There were more than seventy people who attended this mission trip, people from all around the world. There were people from New England and Australia, just to name a couple. Then the vision came back to me again regarding Vietnam. I shared it with the ministries and people on staff. Then the vision started to relight again. I shared the vision with Alan, who is one of the staff from New England. He had been serving with Global Awakening for quite some time. I also talked to Randy Clark, the main pastor and approved him to go Vietnam to equip leaders in Vietnam. This was back in 2012.

From there I headed back to the state and connected with the leaders in Vietnam. We funded the whole event by flipping an investment property. The conference had over 100 leaders from the South and North. With the resources and finances that were entrusted to me, we were able to fund many projects. We did a three day training for 100 leaders in South Vietnam and a three day training in Hai Phong, Vietnam. We had a team of seven people who traveled with us, four from America - Billy, Heidi, Chad, and me - them the team from United Kingdom, which was the Leppitt family of three, his wife Donna and daughter Naomi.

The experience was overwhelming and amazing. We saw people get broken free from addictions and depression. There was also tons of healings throughout the three days of the conference. I remember one incident that I called "the itchy man story". This man from a faraway village had to travel about a day to get to the conference that we were hosting in Hai Phong. He came from a very poor family and he would itch so much throughout the day that he couldn't sleep and eat. He went to see as many doctors as he could find, but no one could cure him. When someone told him about the conference he wanted to go, but because of finances he wasn't able to. But his family insisted. They all gathered the money together and sacrificed to get their father to go, because there was hope that their father would get healing. Because they had exhausted everything else, this was their last hope.

When he came to the conference, Donna asked if anyone need healing and he came to us and she laid her hand on his head. She prayed a prayer to the Father that

He would remove the itchy thoughts from the man's head and I remember laying my hands on his body as well. We didn't know he got healed; it wasn't something that you could see immediately until the next day of the conference.

The next day when we asked if anyone would like to share a testimonial he stood up right away and shared that he had come from far away. He was tearing up as he shared his story that God had healed him. He had been itchy for weeks and did everything he could. Last night he stopped itching and finally had a good night's sleep. Thank God we had the opportunity to fund such an event as that. Thank God that we continued to pursue the vision even though it didn't come through the first time.

I want to leave you with an encouraged heart to pursue the dreams and vision that God has instilled in your heart even if the environment seems daunting. Keep the vision alive when it's in your heart but most importantly, you have to act on it when opportunities arise and let nothing get in your way. Share your vision and stories. You never know if it could be an opportunity for others to accomplish their dreams with your reality. The world is affected by the actions you take. If it wasn't for the constant pursuit of a vision, maybe the itchy man would not have found a cure, I don't know. But I do know that it made a difference in my heart and lifted it to see so many people affected by the visit we made.

Make sure to live life full out and take action to pursue the dreams that God instills in your heart, no matter how many attempts you may need to make. Keep pushing forward and persevere...YOUR dreams and fulfillment of YOUR purpose await you!

## MEET NIKKI NGUYEN...

Nikki Nguyen is a Broker Associate at Keller Williams Realty; her team's name is Nikki Win Team. She has been in the real estate industry for over seventeen years, with years of experience and has been investment consultant to her clients. She had decided to focus on real estate to provide financial freedom and an opportunity of home ownership to help people live the American Dream. Nikki had quickly worked her way to become a top producer in sales for well-known companies such as Coldwell Banker and Keller Williams Realty.

Her savvy negotiations and cutting-edge marketing strategies join uncompromising integrity and serve as the hallmark of Nikki's service. Nikki's primary goal is to help investors reach their dream for financial freedom in real estate in selling their home for top dollars or purchase homes below the market value. She has served for over a decade at her church, E2 and gives all tribute to her success to God. The church has been a huge support to help her grow exponentially mentally, physically, emotionally, and especially spiritually. Her mission trips and relationship with God have been a pivotal encouragement to feed her passion and to live out her big "Why?" which is to help others live out their purpose.

### *Contact Information for Nikki Nguyen:*

Direct:      916-849-2954
Email:      nikkiwinteam@gmail.com
Website:    nikkinguyen.com

# THE AMERICAN DREAM...
## WHO IS THE REAL TEO ORTIZ?
### By Teo Ortiz

The story begins in 1969, in the state of Michoacán in Mexico, in the remote mountains of the Sierra Madre, on the ninth day of the month of November, when he was introduced to the world.

As a small child he had three older siblings who he grew up with. There was nobody else to play with but pets: dogs, chickens, hogs, etc. In those remote mountains he was used to having no electricity. There was no need for it, he says. To be able to see after dark they would have to use a can full of petroleum with a long cloth inside to use as a lamp. He says they use to call it "aparato" - in English apparatus - but is an old style of lamp. Some nights it was fun. He says his dad used to play guitar and sing on the night outside of the house and he used to be so impressed seeing his dad play the guitar. His dad sowed corn and beans every year. In times of rain he sowed the seed to have enough food for the family for the whole year. They lived by the river, where they used to go fishing for shrimp and fish as well. His two older brothers were swimming in the river almost daily. Teo was still too small to swim.

To go to the nearest town would take them twelve hours or more just one way, either walking or on a horseback, they use to come to town about every year only just to pick up necessary things like sugar, salt, or any other condiment. After three years they moved a bit closer to the small town called Arteaga, where they could walk about six hours through the mountains and then catch the bus to the town. Living there a bit closer to town his mom passed away. By this time his dad had just left to the USA when he got the sad surprising news. Because Grandpa and Grandma lived real close in the same ranch, the whole family went to live at the grandparents' house which belonged to Teo's dad's parents, but by this time there were three more small sisters plus the two older brothers and older sisters. There were seven in total. Just imagine how busy the grand parents were with everything from a two-year-old to fifteen-year-old kids.

Because of where they were living was no one to teach. When Teo was nine years old they decided to move to town, where Teo started his first scholar year in 1978. The highest level of education that he accomplished as a child was sixth grade. Living in a small town far from big cities there were not really big opportunities. He started thinking about what the future held for him in that small town. There was a small music band which he made friends with and he thought he would like to learn how to play. His dad bought him an acoustic guitar and he started practicing music. It was something that he really enjoyed doing. Soon enough, the group needed somebody to play guitar in their band and he was very happy to be invited to be part of the group. They played in many cities and small ranches close to town.

In 1989, the whole group made the decision to come to the USA, work hard, and make it big in the music business. At the time of arrival, the whole group ended up staying in a garage where there were already two people living. With the six members of the band added to that, it was difficult, but soon they started playing in a club and moved to a small studio apartment. Teo always had big dreams of becoming successful, but some band members did not like the USA style of living and went back to Mexico right away. Teo started replacing anyone who would leave to keep the band together and continue playing. He started recording records and getting gigs until 2006, when he wanted to spend more time with his wife, daughter, and son.

After the music cycle, he really started thinking about what he was really going to do with his life. He thought to himself, *In what way can I help people, but at the same time make money to provide for my family?* He thought real estate would be one way to do that so he applied himself to study for his real estate license. It was very hard for him maybe because he had not had much schooling and English was his second language. He failed his exam many times, but he did not give up until he passed. He did not know anything about real estate, but he did like the idea of being his own boss and not having to report to anybody. But with no market and with him being new in the business, it was very hard to make it work. Then he found out about how the financial industry worked and everything changed. He saw a huge opportunity in the financial industry and that was where he could help a lot of people with financial education and great strategies that most people did not know existed.

I am excited as I think about my humble beginnings and what has happened in my life. The way I see our world is like this: God has put us here for a reason and it is to do great things for our lives, family, and others. We can all do great things no matter what point in our lives we are at right now. I remember when I first started playing guitar. I really wanted to sing and I asked the singer of the band if he would teach me. He said, "I do not know how to teach you. Just start singing."

Boy, was he right! I am not saying singing is easy. We can all sing, but I am talking about singing in tune, not just screaming off tone. Really, singing is screaming on tone and with feeling, so if we can all sing, we can all do anything great in this wonderful world and have a wonderful life, living our lives to the fullest.

Being able to do something perfectly takes practice. We can all practice to do better for ourselves on whatever we want to be better at. I get so excited when I think about how uniquely God has made all of us. All we have to do is decide what we want and go for it. I believe God has laws in the universe for our own good. Things will be easier for us if we just recognize them and use them to our advantage. For example, no matter if you are a good person or a bad person, if you fall off a ten story building, you will most probably die, which is due to the law of gravity. We do not have to know how the laws of the universe work or why. We just have to recognize them and take advantage of that. We can all plan our lives according to all the rules and laws that God has created and take advantage of all of that. If you have an idea on starting a project or your own business, start whatever you are thinking of doing right now. Do not wait for the perfect time to start. The time is never perfect. You just have to act and things will align your way. Have faith, believe in what you really want, and it will happen for you.

One story that sticks with me and maybe a lot of you have heard is the story of the sower. It says the sower was ambitious and he had excellent seed. This story comes from the Bible and it is a really powerful story that can help us in all aspects of life and business as well. The truth is that we cannot have something right away just because we want it. We have to start with the end in mind but adjust along the way until we get there. In the story of the ambitious sower, his goal was obviously to harvest. But the story says the sower went out to sow the seed and the first part of the seed fell by the wayside and the birds got it. That was the first challenge. So remember, when you are building a business or talking to somebody about an idea that you want accomplish in life, there may be discouragement. There will be birds and when there are birds, you have two options. You can chase birds, start trying to prove a point, or argue about it and try to make them agree with you, but I wouldn't do this. If you chase birds now, you will leave the field, which is going to distract you from your future. And when things are disappointing, all you have to say is, "Isn't that interesting?" and move on.

And the story furthermore says this: the sower kept on sowing. If you keep sowing, you can sow more than what the birds can get because there are only so many birds. Now here is the rest of the story. The sower kept on sowing. That was the secret to the success of the ambitious sower with great seed. This time, the seed fell on rocky ground where the soil was shallow. The rocky ground where the soil is shallow, that is an obstacle not of your making because you have an excellent seed and you are an ambitious sower. Another time, the seed falls on the ground, the little plant starts to grow, and on the first hot day, it withers and dies.

Finally, one person agrees with you but a few days later, somebody talks to you negatively so what happens? The hot weather is going to get some and this is not of your making. All you can say is, "Isn't that interesting?" What can you do? The answer is nothing. You can say, "I am going to try to change this" or "I wouldn't do that" but you can't change those things. That is like rearranging the season. You can't solve that. You just have to cooperate with it and say, "Isn't that interesting?" Some people will not agree with you. You just have to accept that and move on.

Now here is the secret to the ambitious sower with good seed. It says he kept on sowing, but he had to discipline his disappointment. I believe this is a key phrase to use the rest of our lives. We must learn to discipline our disappointment because things happen that are out of our control. Now if we make errors, we must fix them, but in the normal course of things, this is how things are.

The story says the sower kept on sowing and the seed fell on thorny ground. This time the little plant started to grow, but the thorns choked it to death. So remember that the thorns are going to get some of the seed, and that is not of your making. The story even calls the thorns little cares or little distractions.

I set up an appointment with people to show what I can do to help, that I can better their lives if they accept it, but they do not show up or cancel our meeting. I called them and they said, "But the screen door came off the hinges and you just can't let the house fall apart. You have to take some time and fix things up." They said my garage was getting so dirty and that I had to take some time and clean things up.

People let little things cheat them out of big opportunities and make them feel almost helpless. It's just the way it is. All you can say is, "Isn't that interesting?"

But here is the good news. The story says that the sower kept on sowing the seed, kept on sharing the story, kept on giving an invitation - and yes, the invitation can be more powerful a year later than it was the first month. Yes, the story can be more powerful! The story says that finally the seed fell in good ground. Remember this: it always will. If you share an idea long enough, it will fall in the minds and hearts of good people. But you must be like the ambitious sower with good seed. You must discipline your disappointment and keep sowing until happens.

I really want to thank you for reading my chapter in this book. I hope I was able to touch you in a positive way and I sincerely wish you and your family much success in anything you do. Remember, never lose sight of your dream. Decide to never let go and lose hope. Hope drives passion to move forward. Never look back.

## *MEET TEO ORTIZ...*

Teo Ortiz is a proud family man living the American Dream. After beginning life as a musicians' assistant in a small Mexican town, Teo's path led him to an American life and a dedication for helping people through Financial Education. Understanding the true meaning of opportunity and through his appreciation for life and the blessings he has received, Teo is passionate about helping others take care of their families and future.

Teo earned his Real Estate California license in 2011 Over the past years, he has been exposed to highly challenge as measured by even the most seasoned agent's standards. This "trial by fire" education has given him a great deal of intense, critical experience in a short time. He is now an expert resource for his clients, with more compassion and an enhanced perspective on clients. He guides his clients in the financial industry, answering questions and providing consistent communication.

Prior to finance, Teo worked in private education, where he gained priceless experience he applies today. Teo is currently a top producing life agent for Exertus Financial Partners.

*"Having built my life from practically nothing,"* Teo says, *"I cherish the feeling of success in realizing the American Dream and do my utmost to help my clients to achieve their financial goals."*

### *Contact Information for Teo Ortiz:*

Direct Line:    (408) 892-2615

Email:          efptortiz@gmail.com

# BREAK EVERY BARRIER AND MAKE IT *ROCK!*
## By Nichole Peters

### *I Do Understand;*
### *In Fact, I Am One of You!*

Barriers are something every human being will be faced with. The most important factor is how we as humans handle each barrier(s), especially the ones that have caused us pain, shame, guilt, depression, grief, opposition, violence, and abuse. These barriers tend to break us all down—mentally, physically, emotionally, financially, and even spiritually—until we fear there is no longer hope on this beautiful universe to hold on to, no love to share with the world, and no more empathy on today's planet. I know how this feels. Trust me, I am one of you, one out of millions of others on this planet who secretly stay quiet and strong but bitter, with a ton of broken chips on our shoulders, blindsided and sheltered.

What if I told you that you no longer have to live this way? Would you believe me? Maybe so; then, maybe not. I get it, ladies and gentlemen. I understand that anybody can say anything, so what makes my word true? What if I break down step by step the cycles of disaster I faced in different parts of my life and survived to gain the strength to face every barrier and release those horrific chains? In this article, I'll share eleven ways to become free, to believe that you have a purpose to walk straight into your destiny.

### Each One of Our Steps Are Ordered. My Story, My Glory!

I have noticed many times that I have been misunderstood. I realized others just didn't understand and couldn't possibly relate to me. I often said to myself and to my mom (better known as Madear), "What can I do to help others understand why I strongly stand up for others, and why I will keep going no matter what storms I am faced with?"

One day after I'd asked, Madear kept fixing my plate, sat my food on the table, and said, "You're forgetting some things your granny told you, huh?"

I had suffered blows to my head from my violent ex and ended up suffering from a cognitive decline, severe migraines, PTSD, and even short-term memory loss. I was still able to remember many memories of my Shero, my granny, better known as Mamma. I felt blessed to have lived with my grandmother from the time I was born and until the time she took her last breath.

Madear said, "Remember how Mamma used to tell us how people relate to others is to stand up for what you believe in and always use your voice because so many people are voiceless, and never fear or be intimidated by your truth?"

I got up from the table, went over to Madear, put my arms around her, and said, "Own your truth and never be intimidated because of fear of other folks' opinions." I was so excited to finish quoting words of wisdom from my granny.

Madear turned around, smiled, gave me a kiss on my forehead, hugged me, and said, "There's your answer, baby. This is who you are, and even when you were a child, you never settled. Be you. Haven't you realized this is why so many *can* relate to you? Never change because of others who don't see your worth."

You see, I had a hard time dealing with my worth for many reasons. I was a down south, small-town, country girl, born and raised in Bogalusa, Louisiana, in the housing projects called Redmond Heights. Many didn't look at us as ordinary people; they considered us scumbags. I'll never forget the day in class when my teacher asked all her students what they wanted to be. When it came my turn, I replied joyously, "I want to be an author and make people smile and feel great by reading."

My teacher gave me this look I can never forget. The look replayed in mind so much it took me over twenty years just to forgive her. I still talk about it to help others break through, in case this ever happens to them, especially our youth.

As the bell rang for us to go home, my teacher stopped me and said, "Nichole, I'm afraid there's no way you could become a good writer. Why don't you consider becoming something else that doesn't require any writing skills? You know this is your weakest area. Every single day for one full hour you have to be pulled out of class so you can take Title I class in reading comprehension and English."

She had no clue she had just shattered me into pieces. That night before school, I listened to my mom and dad argue for hours. My Madear told my dad she wanted to leave him because she was tired of living a lie. I didn't understand what she was talking about until I got older. The next morning as I was getting dressed for school, I overheard my mom and grandmother talking about my granny's heart condition, which was getting worse. It was a bad day for me, even before walking to school.

I believe the career parent was my angel sent by God. She came in the door, introduced herself, had us to sit in a circle, and she read us this amazing story. She rocked my world, made me smile, and I felt happy. My teacher just had to spoil my moment of happiness by informing me of my inadequacies with a smile on her face as if she was helping me. I knew she did not believe in me, but I believed in her and I set out to change her mind. I vowed to buy her something every week with my $3.00 allowance. I knew Madear didn't have extra money to spend. The money she made took care of her nine kids and any other children in the PJ's that needed to eat, her sickly mother, and her taxi cab for work.

Madear went to the Family Dollar store every Saturday. She would hold my hand while walking in the store and say, "Nichole, pick out a doll or a toy, and don't spend over $3.00." I would opt out of wanting a doll, coloring book, or any small toy so I could please my teacher instead. I'd ask Madear to get my teacher something. I wanted my teacher to like and show me love too. I just wanted her to treat me fairly.

For some odd reason, I faced so much opposition from her. I literally tried my best to prove to her I was just as normal as all the smart students who she showed 99.9% of all her love to, but on that particular day, after she spoke those let-down words to me, I grabbed my backpack recklessly. I was full of anger, shame, and disappointment. I walked with my head down, feeling like a loser. I just didn't understand why any teacher would tell a student this. A child spends 7-8 hours a day with their teacher every Monday-Friday. That is a lot of time for any child to spend with someone, so what teachers say to their students truly matters and can affect their life. For the next seven months, I walked slow like a zombie to her class. I hated it and her. I no longer tried to please her and no longer wanted to be around her.

On my way home, there was a small bridge we had to cross over to get home. I remember stopping at the bridge, pulling off my backpack, and contemplating just diving over. I wanted to take my life at an early age. I wanted to die and float away from all the problems I was facing. I'd had enough. It was bad enough we had to prove to others there was awesomeness where we came from too. There were days a fight would break out before we even made it to school or made it back home from school, but in the Poplas Quarters community, we still had much love for one another.

### When You Are Weak, You Are Beat

As I got older, I suffered many more barriers of defeat. I will never forget losing my granny and father less than a year apart when I was only nineteen years old. I ended up flunking out of college—not once, but twice. I just couldn't stay focused and I was having a hard time dealing with life because I was secretly suffering in agonizing pain and grief.

During my college years, I fell deeply in love with the tutor I was assigned in English. For nineteen months, I thought he was working in an offshore company on the rig in the accounting department with a schedule of two weeks on and two weeks off, unless it was bad weather or selected holidays. By the time I found out he was really a dope dealer, I was already madly in love with him and pregnant.

I was devastated, scared, and afraid, and I couldn't leave him. I regretted staying. I knew it would come back to haunt me, but I also thought love conquered all, and if I stayed because of love, he would eventually change. I was starting to question him about getting a job. I had serious trust issues.

He told me one Thursday evening, "Hey, baby; why don't you come take a trip with me since you think there's someone else in my life? Nik, you never want to go with me. I will never put the love of my life in danger. Come on and go. There's no other girl for me but you, baby doll."

Being just a young girl in love, I decided to take this trip with my man.

Always remember: when you are weak, you are most definitely beat. On that ride, things turned and went extremely bad. I ended up with a gun pointed at my forehead. I had many nightmares remembering how cold the steel from that pistol felt. I was also five months pregnant.

The robber told me, "The only reason I didn't kill you is because you're pregnant. I don't do children. They're our angels."

I thanked God for sparing my life. I vowed to never put myself in danger again and decided to end my relationship. Trust, it wasn't an easy process. I went through pure hell and abuse, and I landed in jail for five days too.

### Instead of Destroying My Life Purpose, I Decided to Live Out My Life Purpose

I always envisioned that one day I was going to be this super-warrior woman, even as a child. I used to dream and play out that one day I was going to save so many people who were going through despair, depression, and abuse. Being raised in a lower-income area, I got to see so many horrible things. I saw people get killed, shot at, cut up, and more. At a young age, I watched drugs and money get transferred from hand-to-hand. I saw women on corners selling their bodies for drugs and money.

Seeing all that, I knew I wanted better. I was ready for a serious change. I was tired of hearing that if you're from the hood, you'd better act hood or else people in your community would think you're weak. I was tired of how society treated people differently because of where they're from or the color of their skin, and putting labels on us before we even got a fair chance to seek our purposes. This alone affects so many young people's mindsets that there is no chance-in-hell they can ever be great. Some believe their only survival mode is the streets or depending on government assistance. I was so tired of being bitter, angry, and frustrated from it all. I decided to take responsibility for my life and do something about it.

## 11 Steps to Break Barriers and Rock!

(1) **B**elieve. You must breakthrough and become a warrior, a fighter, and never give up, no matter what you're facing in life. When you believe in you, your mindset upgrades and becomes one rocking, unstoppable force to be reckoned with. Every chain has no other choice but to break loose.

(2) **A**ppreciate. Thank God you're still breathing and blessed to see the sunshine another day. Happiness and gratitude help us fight mentally, emotionally, and physically. No matter where you are in life, be content and appreciative of Father God's blessings. Many people wish they could be in your shoes. Rock every breath you take. Know that you are a blessing.

(3) **R**esilience. This is how you snatch back control of your life. No matter what setbacks you are faced with, you can face them with the rocking power of ease when you stay resilient. Be optimistic and watch how quickly you recover from all trails. Difficulties won't be so hard once the fruit of self-control is implanted in you.

(4) **R**esponsibility. Don't let yourself be infested with the misery from your past failures, wrong turns in life, or anything you're completely ashamed of. You must accept that you made those choices. Apologize to yourself first; own your truth and your shame. Let go and let God. Share your story as a wake-up call, not to brag or be boastful, but in hopes you will see that life is what we make it when we try to accept our downfalls. Rock not your mistakes, but your lessons learned on the roadmap to becoming a better you.

(5) **I**dentity. The first way to identify who you are is to look in a mirror and start staying true to who you are because everyone else is taken. Rock who you were born to be. The way you look at yourself matters. Stay completely confident in knowing it is all

right to be you and to value you. Do not let the pressure of today's society turn you into something you are not. People relate to others better when they know they're authentic.

(6) **E**xecute. Once you have worked on all the above, take action and make plans on how to move forward. Write down your goals in life and start accomplishing them one by one. You have the power to become who you were sent to be. I was still able to "Believe In My Dreams", even after being told I couldn't be a great speaker because of my cognitive decline. I am now a sought-after motivational speaker, better known as "The Breakthrough Catalysts". I was told I couldn't be a great author, but with the Lord's blessing, I did become a writer, a #1 bestselling author, and an international publisher.

I was told I wouldn't be a great mother. I watched my kids, who suffered with disabilities, graduate with a 3.0 or higher, and they are now on their way to rocking on success' door. I was told the only men I would cling to were street thugs who beat their women. I now have one amazing, hardworking soulmate who has never put his hands on me. I was told I wouldn't be great at anything, that I would return to the ruthless street life and the things that came with it. I've learned how to ignore their opinions of me by believing in me.

Right now, I need to stop for one minute and just shout, *HALLELUJAH*! It's been over a decade and I haven't looked back. All of my biggest accomplishments have come to fruition and have manifested. So can yours. Dream big and go be great!

(7) **R**elentlessly. Stay persistent on your task. You might fall down fifty times, but get back up fifty-one. My children are my most precious gifts from God. When I looked at them, I refuse to break, or turn cold and unmerciful, or throw a pity party. My fight for life got stronger. I grew up on government assistance most of

my life. I wanted this generational darkness to stop carrying on in my family. Being on welfare made me see I was so much than that, to not limit myself to settle for a few hundreds of dollars. Being on food stamps helped me appreciate how blessed I am now to walk in the store and spend cash on food.

With very limited resources, I took some losses going for my dreams. I no longer could afford my rent or my car. I lost both trying to push forward. It isn't easy, but FIGHT no matter how tired you get. Continue breaking through your darkest setbacks so your light can come back and shine. Don't get tired, get motivated. Every L (loser) can turn to a W (winner), to become a strong, independent person. We're rocking this together!

(8)  Self-Esteem. By now, with all the different changes, you might go through a phase like I went through. I thought, once I changed, put myself in positive situations, and was finally on the right track, that I should be feeling joyous about myself. Let me warn you: there are people who are ready to tear you down. There are users who want your visions, and some who will turn on you and bad-mouth you, especially after they get what they want from you. You'll start to think, "What's wrong with me?" I'll tell you: there's nothing wrong with you. Ninety percent of the time, it's them. They want you to feel as if you aren't supposed to be where you are. Don't fall into this trap; instead, rise above it. You must love yourself first before you can love anyone else. Look in the mirror again and say, "I've got this, so let me rock this!"

(9)  Obviate. By the time you get here, you might have removed a lot of baggage in your life. To persevere, you must get rid of all the blockers. You'll carry less weight on your shoulders once you learn ways to prevent yourself from getting stuck and eliminate the problems. Let go of trying to please others and just love others, regardless of how they feel toward you. The barrier

and chains can no longer hold you down once you rock away unwanted issues.

(10) <u>F</u>aith. I put all my trust in my highest power, Who is God. Jeremiah 29:11 says, "For I know the plans I have for you," declares the LORD, "plans to prosper you and not to harm you, plans to give you hope and a future." The Almighty knows what plans He has for you. He is the Source to pull you out from of danger that threatens the purpose He created you for. He is your Healer and your Waymaker. He wants to be a glorious light. Praying and meditation are key factors in how your life will be lived daily. The best relationship I ever experienced was getting to know God. He delivered me up from so many snares. I knew it was Him Who rocked my very soul.

(11) <u>F</u>reedom. Whooo! By now you should feel good and FREE. All your dried-up bones should be overflowing and healed abundantly. You can defeat all the odds stacked against you. FIGHT. Let the warrior in you battle back against every nightmare from your inner and exterior critics. I knew one day I would get to this point, and I am counting on you to do the same. Why?

I did become "Nikki Woman", the black soul-sista version of Wonder Woman who wanted to save anyone feeling downtrodden or going through distress and violence. I birthed my warrior mindset. The bracelet I wear every single day is truly my protection. It reads, "GOD IS BIG ENOUGH."

Warrior up and break every barrier and chain now! You are loved. Now let's go rock the world!

## MEET NICHOLE PETERS ...

Nichole Peters is an international motivational speaker and author of the best-selling book, *A Woman of Love, Power, and Respect*, as well as the #1 best-selling book, *Women Warriors Who Make It Rock*. Nichole is the Founder and CEO behind many best-selling authors from her company, *Believe In Your Dreams Publishing*.

Nichole is determined to teach downtrodden women and youth the power of self-love, purpose, and rocking ambition through workshops, conferences, retreats, and events. She was born and raised in Bogalusa, Louisiana (63 miles north of New Orleans). She has experienced many hardships in life, but has never lost hope that she would one day serve a greater purpose. As a result, God has blessed her with four amazing, beautiful children, sent her the love of her life, and revealed to her the potential to be a ready writer.

Over the past years, Nichole has garnered a social media following of almost 60,000. She has also been featured in *The Huffington Post, VoiceAmerica*, Amazon, *In The Red, The Motivational Lounge, Rush Hour For Success*, and *Empowering Women Transforming Lives*.

She is currently setting up her own TV and radio network called Believe In Your Dreams Productions. Her shows will start airing August 1, 2018, called *The Motivational Lounge* and *Women Warriors Table Talk,* powered by Believe In Your Dreams TV Network.

## *Contact Information for Nichole Peters:*

Email:        www.believeinyourdreamspublishing@gmail.com
Facebook:     www.facebook.com/luvpowerrespect.com
Twitter:      www.Twitter.com/luvpowerrespect
Amazon:       www.Amazon.com/NicholePeters
Telephone:    (813) 309-2778

# GRIEF'S GATEWAY TO A NEW LIFE
## By Dr. Michelle Peticolas

I found my mother in the kitchen crying. A jar of peanut butter lay smashed on the floor. As I took her in my arms to console her, she sobbed, "I just can't do it anymore. I can't see; I can't hear; I have no balance. I can't live like this."

A chill shivered through me – a physical premonition of what was to come. Six months later both my mother and father were dead – my father from Alzheimer's and then my mother from breast cancer.

In the time of their decline, I faced a big learning curve. I had little knowledge or experience with death. As a result, I made many mistakes and choices that later filled me with regret. In the process of my healing, I discovered that although the loss of my parents punched a big hole in my world, it also contained the seeds of a new one. Grief was my gateway to a new life purpose.

It was the end of 1997 and I was home for Christmas after recently moving to California from New Jersey. I was at the start of a new chapter in my life – new friends, new relationship, new work, and new location. My parents, in contrast, were ending theirs.

My father was in a VA nursing home. He had pneumonia, a common occurrence in late stage Alzheimer's. The decision had been made to stop all treatment and transition him into hospice care.

My mother had been my father's caregiver for many years and was at the end of her rope – thin, exhausted, blind in one eye, deaf in one ear, half her face paralyzed from brain surgery. She was also having recurrences of breast cancer. It was a difficult Christmas.

I went to visit my father at the VA. I sat and read to him from a book of folktales as he struggled to breathe. Peter, Paul and Mary sang "I'm Leaving on a Jet Plane" from an ancient cassette player. It felt surreal. I hated the institutional setting: the echoing hallways, antiseptic smells, green walls and the hollow-eyed inmates lined up in wheelchairs against the wall.

I visited my father once over the holidays, maybe twice, and then drove ninety minutes away to be with my boyfriend.

The next day, my mom called to say that she thought this was it. But I had just gotten to my boyfriend's and didn't want to return. I didn't believe her, didn't want to believe her. I went to a museum with my boyfriend instead. That evening, my mother called to tell me that my dad had died. Did I want to come back to see the body? What? No, why would I want to do that?

I went the next day to a family meeting at the mortuary to schedule the date of my father's memorial. The family got into a huge argument over which day to hold it. I wanted to leave as soon as possible. I wanted to get back home and back to my life. I wanted to get away.

Later I learned that fighting is one of the ways people handle loss when they don't know how to grieve. It's an automatic survival response because losing a loved one is experienced by the body as a threat to its survival. Fleeing is another survival response.

We were all relieved when my father died. It was horrible watching a once brilliant man gradually reduced to a wheelchair and nonsensical strings of words. I felt he had been released; that we all were.

Then, a month later, I got the news that my mother was going into surgery. Her breast cancer had spread to her liver and was now blocking her intestines. My boyfriend and I were in the middle of house hunting and my current living situation was getting crazier by the day. I hardly registered the seriousness of my mother's situation--that she could die on the operating table. Thankfully, she didn't.

My boyfriend and I went back East, once our housing was settled, to visit my mom and move the rest of our things to California. She seemed fine, like her old self. I was in complete denial.

My mother went through two protocols of chemotherapy and stopped treatment. The chemotherapy made her too sick. What was the point of living if you felt that awful?

I flew back to give my sisters a break from caring for my mom. I had these glorious notions about the sacredness of dying, about the conversations I planned to have with her. The reality was a blaring radio, cats peeing in all the corners of the house, and my brother and his wife hiding in their room paralyzed with fear about what would happen to them after she died. The tension was so thick you could cut it with a knife.

I tried to remain strong, efficient, and in control. I avoided the hard subjects to spare my mom – or so I believed. On a brief overnight to the city to visit some friends, my back went into spasms. I cried all night, quietly so I wouldn't wake them. I felt a wreck and it had only been ten days. Frightened by my physical reaction and my tumultuous feelings, I flew back to California, knowing I would probably never see my mom again.

Two weeks later, she went into a coma. The nurse said it was a matter of days. But I had a TV show scheduled the following weekend with all my guests lined up and I didn't want to cancel.

I thought I should go back, but took hold of my sister's words about that not being necessary and to remember the way she was.

I was ambivalent. I promised myself that if she was still alive after the weekend, I would go back.

Then I started getting emails from my sister about my mother hanging on and the nurse wondering what was holding her back. It finally dawned on me that it was ME who was holding her back. I burst into tears from the realization and shouted up to the sky, "It's okay, Mom, for you to go. It's not about me. You can go." She died that night.

I still wanted to do the TV show and had another argument with my sisters about scheduling Mom's memorial date. They accommodated my schedule, but the TV show, wouldn't you know, was a disaster. The audio levels were set wrong and all you could hear of the Middle Eastern band on my show was the rattle of a tambourine. It was a hard lesson about what is really important.

I was mess. There were long crying jags and further skirmishes with my sisters. I felt bad about not going back for my mother's death, for my father's death, for the missed opportunities to show up. I had utterly failed Facing Death 101.

Like a student in college, I decided to do an extra credit project to redeem myself. I decided in the wake of my mother's departure to make a film about death. I was going to change the world, to start the conversation, to help people be prepared so they didn't make the mistakes I did!

It was a life-changing decision. It gave my parents' deaths a new meaning and it gave me purpose and a way to make amends. It also turned out to be a way to heal my grief.

I stopped running from my feelings and got curious. Death was such a huge event. Why had I not been more prepared? Why was it such a secret? My filmmaking became my vehicle for finding out.

Although I had been producing community TV shows for five years, I had no experience making a documentary. The prospect scared me out of my mind. I had no budget, no crew, no equipment, and no idea how to begin. Who was I to be making a film?

I started alone, discretely, and quickly realized that filmmaking is a communal activity. The footage I shot in my first interview left the subject mostly out of the frame because I was too busy asking questions to check the viewfinder.

Two important things, however, resulted from this initial effort: One, I found the courage to continue. The woman I interviewed told me that the loss of her spouse gave her courage. She realized that nothing could be as awful. So why worry? Two, my film had gone from thought to action. I was officially making my film.

I borrowed equipment from the TV station where I taped my shows and convinced a series of aspiring cameramen to shoot my interviews for lunch and credits. Over the next ten years, while working part-time at a law firm, I pieced together a three part documentary series called *Secrets of Life and Death*. The series explores facing death, the gifts and trials of caregiving, and the journey of grief.

Through the process of creating the films, I began to understand death and loss in a new and empowering way. I joined hospice and started leading bereavement groups.

After completing my first two films in 2008, I began screening them around the San Francisco Bay Area. This brought my work to the attention of the Lloyd Symington Foundation, which awarded me three consecutive grants to take the films to the cancer community. I learned about facing death and loss every day.

I now coach professional women struggling with grief. I find that, like me, they believe they need to be strong and tamp down their feelings. This makes it hard to let go of the loss and affects all their relationships and how they show up in the world.

In my grief work I have identified three powerful secrets that make grieving not only more manageable, but also a gateway to a new life:

## 1. Allow Your Feelings

Like many of us in this Western culture, I learned to control my feelings and to deny loss, replace it or run away. What my parents' deaths taught me was that being strong and tamping down feelings could hurt me and hurt my relationships with my family.

As I said earlier, the body perceives loss of a close relationship as a threat to survival. Hormones are released from the pituitary to prepare the body to fight, flee or freeze.[1] This is useful when facing a saber-toothed tiger or angry assailant, but not so helpful when dealing with grief. It does not address the problem. It does, however, explain all the arguments I had with my sisters over scheduling memorial services and also my tendency to run back home to California every time things got too scary.

Because the survival response has no practical function in grief, the hormones are not released and this can lower the immune system and affect health. Dr. Mostofsky, from The Harvard School of Public Health, did a study and found that

---

[1] Powledge, Tabitha M. *Your Brain: How You Got It and How It Works.* New York: Charles Scribner's Sons, 1994. Novitt-Moreno, Anne. *How Your Brain Works.* Emeryville, CA: ZiffDavis Press, 1995.

people who had experienced a significant loss were twenty-one times more likely to experience a heart attack than those who hadn't. [2]

Allowing feelings does not mean endless weeping and wailing. When emotions are truly allowed to release, they will process through fairly quickly. "Truly allowing" requires thought mastery - which brings me to the second powerful secret for dealing with grief:

## 2.    Master or Change Your Thoughts

The thoughts I had after my parents' deaths were upsetting. I kept thinking about how I could have done things better and why I didn't. While making my film, I discovered that EVERYONE makes mistakes. It is impossible to be perfect and nothing you do can change the fact that your loved one is dying. I gradually began to forgive myself and to accept that mistakes are part of the learning process.

This learning has enabled me to help others. When one of my housemates got word that his sister was in the hospital and in serious condition, I urged him to go home. He wanted to wait, to see what developed. I said, "Don't wait." He took my advice and was home with family when she died.

The human brain is powerful in its capacity to think symbolically, to envision and problem solve. This power, however, also comes with a liability. The brain can replay the past and imagine a future. The body perceives these thoughts to be real. When these thoughts are disturbing, depressing, and hopeless, the body reacts. You can check this out for yourself by observing your own mind after an emotional event. As the mind recalls the

---

[2] Mostofsky, E. *Circulation: Journal of the American Heart Association,* published online Jan. 9, 2012.

specific details of the upset, it will set off a fresh emotional response as though it were actually happening.

Disturbing, repetitive thoughts can keep the body emotionally revved up for a long time. If you stop the thoughts, the emotions will process through the body in two minutes or less.

Sometimes it is difficult to stop thoughts, even for a master meditator. I find that it helps to focus attention on the physical sensations in the body, e.g. choked throat, faster heartbeat, jittery limbs, tight stomach, etc. By paying attention and breathing the body will gradually relax.

After the emotions are released, it is helpful to come up with a new story - a story that empowers and uplifts instead of victimizes.

This is exactly what I did with my parents' deaths. I shifted from feeling bad about myself to seeing my mistakes as the impetus to make my films and help others. We learn from our mistakes. That's how we grow. It is important to remember, always.

The last secret for dealing with grief is:

### 3. Savor Support

After my mom died, I had a huge need to tell the story of my losses and hear the stories of others. Fortunately, I went to a group retreat right after my mother's memorial and found plenty of people willing to listen and share. It felt so reassuring to be heard and understood and to know there were things I could do.

Humans are social animals. We are physically designed to bond to one another. It's Mother Nature's way of insuring our species' survival. The human baby takes years to mature, to become self-sufficient. Oxytocin is one of the hormones Mother

Nature uses to keep Mom and Dad around long enough for the baby survive.[3] Oxytocin is a feel good hormone that releases whenever we hug, gaze into each other's eyes, or nurse a baby.

When a loved one dies, social bonds are broken. The loss of bonding is experienced as a threat to survival because biologically, it actually is. The mortality rate for a surviving spouse can be has high at 66% within the first three months of the loss[4]

The loss of a loved one causes an oxytocin deficit. It feels awful. This is Mother Nature's way of nudging us to bond again. I felt the need to tell the story of my mother's loss because I craved social connection. My body needed it.

Savoring support means to take it in slowly with awareness. Resist the gluttonous desire for attention. I didn't know this in my first go around. Fortunately there were so many people at the retreat that I didn't swamp anyone.

It is good to have plenty of people to turn to for solace, and also good to limit their exposure. People do not need nor can they "solve" grief. All they need do is listen. Putting a limit on the amount of time encourages the "savoring" and is less likely to overwhelm your support person.

The other thing to remember about savoring support is to seek hugs from people you trust. Encourage those oxytocin boosts at least five times a day.

---

[3] *Lee HJ, Macbeth AH, Pagani JH, Young WS (June 2009).* "Oxytocin: the great facilitator of life". *Progress in Neurobiology.* **88** (2): 127–51.
[4] Boyle, P. J., Feng, Z., & Raab, G. M. (2011). Does Widowhood Increase Mortality Risk? Epidemiology, 22(1), 1-5.

Connection after a loss can be a challenge for many because of our cultural tendency to rely on a single person for most of our social needs. Many of us don't do community much unless or until we are single. When a significant other dies or leaves, we often discover there are few people to turn to.

Now is a good time to review your social networks and identify whom you might depend upon. Who could you turn to in need? Can you rely on them? Isn't it time to add a few more?

A friend of mine who lost her husband two years ago expected the support of two very close friends. When they arrived at her home simultaneously, they were instantly attracted to each other and quickly abandoned her in order to enjoy their newfound bliss. It's a story of caution. Grief can and does change your address book.

Some people may need professional help to handle their grief because all losses are connected in the mind. Current grief often churns up earlier losses that have never been fully healed. This is where I come in. I teach people how to allow their feelings, change their story from victim to empowerment, and get the support they need to create a new life after loss.

More information about my work and how my clients are supported during a time of loss and grief can be found on my website: www.secretsoflifeanddeath.com. A complimentary mini-book, *Essentials for Grieving Well,* can be download for free.

## *MEET MICHELLE PETICOLAS, Ph.D...*

Dr. Michelle Peticolas has been nationally recognized for her unique contributions to individuals, groups and organizations in the field of death and loss for more than 17 years.

She earned her Ph.D. in Sociology and Clinical Psychology from Indiana University where she received a 4-year National Institute of Mental Health Fellowship.

Dr. Peticolas leads workshops and presentations for universities, hospitals, and professional organizations throughout the United States, including UCSF, UC Berkeley, The National Hospice and Palliative Care Organization, Sutter Health, Kaiser Permanente, and The Commonwealth Club of San Francisco. Her presentations attract diverse audiences interested in enhancing and developing their awareness, skills and effectiveness in managing and coping with grief.

Dr. Peticolas' unique program, *Release Your Grief and Thrive,* designed for professional women, has received praise for its structure, design and powerful impact on those navigating the challenges of death and loss.

She has appeared on Voice America's *Good Grief* and *Leadership Stars*, KDIA's *Aging By The Bay*, BBM Global Network's *Courage-2-Overcome*, KPFA's *Women's Magazine* and Money 1055's *Rush Hour for Success.*

In 2010 she received the first of three grants from the Lloyd Symington Foundation to present unique and creative approaches to grief, trauma and loss to cancer organizations across the country including: the National Cancer Support Community, The Wellness Center, Gilda's Club, CancerCare, and The Markstein

Cancer Center. In January 2016, she spoke at Commonweal's International Conference on New Directions in Cancer Care.

An award-winning filmmaker, Dr. Peticolas produced the 3-part documentary series, *Secrets of Life and Death*. Her films are viewed in university classrooms throughout the United States, Canada, Australia and New Zealand to inspire discussion and encourage new responses to life's endings.

### *Contact Information for Dr. Michelle Peticolas:*

Direct Line:    (510)529-4806
Email:          mp@secretsoflifeanddeath.com
Website:        www.secretsoflifeanddeath.com

# BREAKTHROUGH TO FREEDOM AND JOY - THE SECRETS TO POWERING RECOVERY, WELLNESS AND SUCCESS TO ACHIEVE WHAT YOU DESIRE
### *By Jon Taber*

What do freedom and joy feel like? Do you regularly experience them, or are they only fleeting memories from your childhood?

For example, did you feel freedom and joy when you started to walk and explore the world like a big person, talk, ride a bike, sit at the big table with adults, go to school on your own, read your first book, and make new friends? Take a few moments and recall what happened. Hopefully the experiences made you feel powerful and unstoppable, able to breakthrough any barrier. Adults call these uplifting and life-changing emotions freedom and joy. If you have not experienced it yourself, imagine and believe it is true.

I feel freedom and joy as a warm lightness in my upper abdomen and heart that radiates out to every part of my body. During those times I'm more energetic, carefree, loving, and healthy. I attract opportunities and like-minded people who want to be with me.

When I worry or feel resistance, fear, or other barriers, I get a cold, sinking feeling in my gut and my energy drops. When that happened in the past, I would try to shut down and hide from those limitations.

Good news! Breakthrough thinking and uplifting behavior can reignite the feelings of freedom and joy because all barriers are illusions, just like the mirage of a lake in a burning hot desert. How do I know? I learned the hard way, many, many times.

**Doomsday**

Life-changing barriers started building up on September 11, 2001 and erupted like a volcano on April 2007. I was seated at our dining room table, working on our income tax return while recalling an ever-increasing pile of bad events in the following order:

- Failure of a $20 million computer company of which I was CEO following the terror attacks of September 11, 2001. Judy and I had to declare bankruptcy and start over again.

- My mother's health was declining, and Judy was diagnosed with diabetes. I started to have problems with my immune system, extreme joint pain, and loss of muscle coordination. Judy had a mild stroke. I experienced pancreatitis and severe Crohn's Disease. I'm on strong morphine five times a day for pain plus a huge list of other medications for my weakening health. I had to quit working. Now Judy is on oxygen and can barely walk.

- My mother died. Judy and I agreed to move to Vancouver, WA to stay with our son and his family so that they could take care of us. We were moving the next week.

The next thing I knew I was driving my car and I didn't know why or where. Blurry road signs were zooming by. Slowing down a bit, I realized I was on highway 99 going toward Stockton, about forty miles from our home in Sacramento. I reached for my cell phone, but it wasn't there. My wallet, driving glasses, and shoes were missing too. Confused and scared, I barely had enough awareness to stop, turn the car around, and start for home. I almost made it.

I ran a red light and a police car behind me pulled me over. The officer rapidly approached me, saying, "Mr. Taber, your wife is worried about you. We've been looking for you for several hours. We've called for an ambulance to take you to a hospital."

Doctors determined I had experienced a stroke while at home and had left, taking only my car keys and driving in a semiconscious state for over eighty miles. At any moment I could have crashed and killed someone.

Arriving at the hospital, I was beyond the safe timeline for a clot-breaking stroke treatment. I would have to recover on my own with the following issues: over 35% loss of muscle strength and coordination on my right side and loss of vocabulary, memory, and ability to speak and do what I'm thinking.

### The Downward Spiral Continues

Judy and I moved to WA and Judy's health continued to decline. She was diagnosed with heart failure and given a short time to live. I suffered another stroke and lost more abilities. I was feeling depressed and hopeless.

Shortly before she died on May 5, 2008, Judy said, "Don't give up. Promise me that you will find another woman to take my place. You will be fine."

Judy died while talking to me in our bedroom. I couldn't believe it! My loving wife of forty-two years was gone. My world crashed around me. I felt so alone.

I tried to put on a good face, but my behavior became more erratic. I couldn't remember my grandson's name and other important things about my life. My family kicked me out after I made too many bad decisions. I had an emotional breakdown. Regardless, a friend in Sacramento agreed to let me stay with him for a couple of weeks.

One evening while my friend was gone, I sat on his patio writing down everything wrong with me. It took both sides of three

8.5" X 11" pages. Despair was pouring out of me. I felt beaten and worthless.

I finally stopped and asked the ultimate question: do I end it all now, or keep going?

The answer came in a flash of light and clarity. "Keep going. Never give up! You will find ways to recover and lead a healthy life. We are counting on you to complete the work you and Judy started. Millions of people will benefit. You can do this."

I sat in stunned silence, not sure what to believe or do. I was sweating and shivering. Did I just imagine what happened?

Suddenly I was inspired to take the sheets of paper into the bathroom, rip them into small bits, and flush them down the toilet. As I watched the last shreds of paper disappear in a swirl of water, I felt immense relief in my heart and a renewed since of my personal worth, even though I didn't know why. I started to warm up and I stopped shaking. My mind was focused on one thing: get into bed and start over again in the morning.

### Revival

The next day I made a focused commitment to survive, recover and thrive by doing three things:

1. Using the personal transformation system that Judy and I created between 1982 and 2006. It was unfinished but the strategies, tools, and processes were advanced enough to serve my needs. The rest of my story in this book tells you a summary of the results and how it works.

2. High quality balanced meals and good water and other beverages prepared by my host and roommate, a world class chef.

3. I returned to work and strived to create a normal social life.

Within a year, all Crohn's Disease and significant stroke symptoms disappeared so I discontinued using morphine and all other medications. I was normal and useful again. I started on a new career path, married the wonderful Nancy Schaal, and used what I learned help individuals and organizations break through barriers with freedom and joy.

## Fast Facts about Key Things I Used to Recreate My Life

The foundation of my recovery, wellness, and success is based on personal "secrets" that describe how I believe life and creativity works. I'm giving you permission to use them too.

Many of my ideas are controversial and so you may want to keep them to yourself until you have tested and proven they work.

Finally, please understand that I summarized the ideas to fit within this book chapter. For more detailed information, please contact me and I will gladly share what you need to know.

***Secret #1** - Scientists Think That Everything in Life May Be a Holographic or Energy Projection of Our Consciousness*

I believe our true nature is formless source energy and that we are spiritual beings having a human experience. Further, I believe that moment-to-moment thoughts and emotions define our beliefs and intentions which in turn infuse, interact with, and influence the quantum energy field and reality all around us. In other words, we control what happens to us.

Scientists are coming to believe that our reality and everything we perceive is a holographic or energetic projection of our consciousness. It works by oscillating like a swinging pendulum, strobe light, or firefly flashing in and out of existence innumerable times, every moment using energetic forms or blueprints to create our bodies and all life experiences. Energy, frequencies, and vibration are the building blocks of the universe and your life.

Half of the time we are formless and the material world is illusory to some extent. The other half of the time we are guiding the manifestation or materialization of energy, frequencies, and vibration to create our bodies and life. All of this is experienced by us as a stream of consciousness and life experiences.

**Secret #2** -*Life Is Organized Energy*

When directed by thought, particles of matter assemble using their own intelligence. We are related and linked to all matter and vibrations in the universe. Thoughts have energy, intelligence, and a life force of their own. Each thought has a specific frequency of vibration. Each frequency is information. You are a vibrational being in a vibrational universe.

**Secret #3** - *Life Experience is a External Projection From Our Mind, Influenced by Over 70,000 Waking Thoughts Each Day. Learn to Control It with the Right Mindset*

Every waking day you produce tens of thousands of thoughts that affect everything; your desires, imagination, creative visualizations or active images, emotions, feelings and self talk, plus your commitment to learning, change, and growth. The trick to getting what you want in life is to start with a proper mindset.

Some people think that mindset is a belief, attitude, disposition, or behavior. While that is true, there is more to it - much more. I believe that the right mindset can be a powerful stream of consciousness that facilitates the deliberate creation of what we want, need, and desire. In other words, *the right mindset creates a better life.*

There are dozens of potential mindsets. I teach people how to produce and control the most important ones to fit their unique personality and needs.

You can enable a desired mindset or stream of consciousness using 7 Stages of Thought and Action to engage and influence your behavior. With practice, some of the 7 stages can be done simultaneously or compressed for simple and faster results.

The following is a summary of the *7 Stages*:

**Stage 1 - Be Self-Aware**

It's all about how you perceive and relate to our vibrational world. Your personality thrives when you achieve vibrational alignment with the authentic you, your higher self, inner being, soul, God, or whatever name you give to your source. When you are in alignment you are calm, full of positive energy, power, and stamina. You are healthier, you look and feel good. Like-minded people are attracted to you.

While you are in alignment, you know your "WHY": why you were born and why you do what you do. You are aware of your unique strengths, power, thoughts, beliefs, motivations, and emotions.

Accurate self-awareness gives you the ability to better understand others in your life and how together you can achieve mutual goals and objectives by trusting and working in concert with each other and not in conflict. Resistance and blocks are fewer and solutions to problems flow to you whenever you need them. There is abundance all around you and you uplift others. Positive momentum accelerates and produces whatever you want, desire, or need with fewer exceptions and effort. All of the other alignments can be achieved faster. The key is to breathe deeply, relax, love yourself, and follow your bliss. You will feel freedom and joy.

### Stage 2 - Produce Positive Emotions

Tune your sensory receptivity, perceptions, and interpretations to know without a doubt that what you desire is already created in a non-physical form, waiting for your personal energy, frequency, vibration, and intention to match it. What you express and believe as a want or desire will come to you when you are ready to receive it - not before.

Vividly recall some of your most pleasing and uplifting life experiences and then imagine new, joyful, and expanding life experiences. Believe it without a doubt or resistance.

### Stage 3 - Set Clear Intentions

Accept the fact that the Universe understands what you mean, not your words. Your emotions and feeling are the best indicators of what you really mean or intend. Learn to sense and interpret your emotions in almost everything you do.

### Stage 4 - Visualize Complete and Successful Outcomes

Achieve and maintain undivided focus, clarity, meaning, and alignment with your intention. See what you want or desire in your mind as a detailed, full color image. Bring it up close to you and rotate it so that you can see all aspects. Make it move as in real life and link a positive feeling to it for maximum impact. Believe it and you will see it.

### Stage 5 - Allow, Don't Resist

Get out of your own way! Resistance kills creativity or sends you on unproductive detours that waste your time, energy, and opportunities. Let go of control (there really isn't any; the best you can do is influence something).

Listen to your inner guidance and take the path of least resistance. How do you know if you are on the right path? It feels good, you are happy, joyful, and unconcerned about what is happening or what comes next.

Know you are worthy and good enough to have what you desire and then strive to create value in everything you do.

### Stage 6 - Produce Right Thinking and Actions

Your thoughts become things, actions, or performance. Make the majority of your 70,000 daily thoughts positive and uplifting. Repeat a desired thought at least 35-50 times per day. Believe it with all of your power. Make it a high priority and never give up on your idea.

### Stage 7 - Feel Good About It

Whether you know or believe it, you are always on the right life path. Just believe that things are always working out for you and eventually they will. Don't worry; be joyful and thrive regardless of what is going on around you. Remember, what you are experiencing right now is old news; it is in the past and has no real effect. Create a new experience that you want and enjoy.

**Secret #4** - *The Reality Transformer™ Can Help You Make Sense of Life, Overload, Complexity, and Confusion.*

It is a visual tool and thought process that directs your attention and consciousness while it facilitates your creativity and physical manifestations. Following is a picture of a Reality Transformer with key words that are too small to read.

**Transform**

**Evaluate Present & Past**

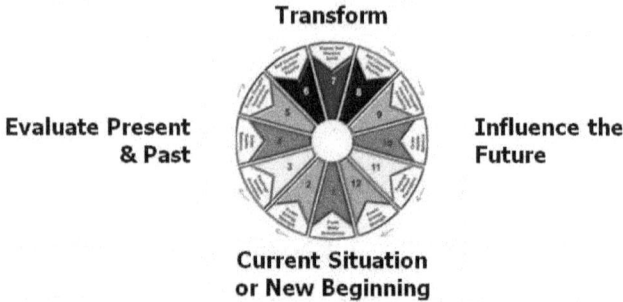

**Influence the Future**

**Current Situation or New Beginning**

How it works - The Reality Transformer integrates our intuition and rational thinking skills and deals with:

1. The current situation or current reality (red). This is reality as we perceive it, at this moment in time. It is ever changing and is influenced by everything in our environment, other people and ourselves.

2. The immediate past (the left side, from orange to a part of violet). This is everything that happened after, or during the past current situation or current reality.

3. A "gap" (the middle of violet) where creativity occurs, desired changes emerge, and we start to create a new potential future.

4. A potential future (the right side, from a part of violet to orange). This is a picture of a new reality that we are creating in our mind that will pull us into a new and different current situation or current reality.

There are twenty-two templates with key words that you can use to create the life you desire. I would love to give you a personal demonstration of how to use it.

**Secret #5** - *Creative Tension Powers Your Creativity and Manifestations*

## CURRENT REALITY → VISION OF A NEW REALITY
## CREATIVE TENSION

*Creative tension is a potential energy like a stretched rubber band that will release the energy when it is let go. Your vision of the future must be stronger than the present or past to create what you desire!*

The Reality Transformer uses creative tension to help you imagine and create all required parts of your new reality.

### What This All Means to You

The most important things I can say to you in this short chapter are:

"Don't be fooled by false assumptions that resistance and barriers are created by other people or situations over which you have little or no control. *All resistance and barriers are self imposed!* They are excuses for failures when we don't realize and follow our inner guidance.

You create and influence everything you experience. The Universe or other people are not doing to you. You can empower recovery, wellness and success to achieve what you desire.

You can feel freedom and joy every day and I can help you do it. Believe it.

## *MEET JON TABER...*

Jon Taber is a forty-year founder and CEO of seventeen organizations in eleven different fields, including medical, entertainment, technology, wholesale/retail and lifestyle. Jon has been a consultant to Fortune 1,000 corporations, federal, state, local, and military and non-profit organizations; speaker at thirty-six colleges and universities; executive coach, consultant, mentor, and trainer to over 5,000 leaders and managers.

Jon is the author of *Child's Play,* plus four forthcoming books: *Win with This Astonishing and Powerful 7-Stage Mindset*; *How to Survive, Thrive and Achieve Your Dreams*; *22 Keys to Leadership Success*: and *Who Are You? What Is Your Life Purpose?*

Jon is co-host of *The CEO Leadership Corner* on Live Strong America—Radio to Inspire at: livestrongamerica.com, and is a frequent special guest on KSAC MONEY 105.5 FM, Rush Hour for Success.

### *Contact Information for Jon Taber:*

Email:        jon@jontaber.com

# FROM DISGRACE TO VICTORY
## By Rev. Thabiti

As a young black kid, it seemed like everything I saw about black people made me feel ashamed and embarrassed. This is simply because of the way the American culture depicts them. The people I had to look up to were the slaves in recent history: Aunt Jemima, Buckwheat of the TV show *The Little Rascals* or Kid Dyn-o-mite of the show *Good Times*. I was told that because I was black, I needed to be in sports or entertainment in order to make it. I vehemently rejected this notion and felt deeply that one day I would be able to break this barrier and compete fairly using my brain and succeed on my own merit.

From birth until I was ten years old I lived in Philadelphia in a mostly black community, where I saw cops almost daily do horrifying things to innocent blacks. In fact, because of this, it is my strong opinion that cell phone cameras are the worst thing to ever happen to all police departments because now a few of these extreme abuses are finally being caught on tape.

My parents worked extremely hard to move me and my siblings into the New Jersey suburbs when I was in the fifth grade for fear that I would end up in a gang. From then on, I found myself being the only black kid in my class. I was not allowed to play games with the other kids like Spin the Bottle nor was I allowed to date any of the white girls and they most clearly and definitely wanted no romantic involvement with me whatsoever in any way, shape, or form. When I would walk to school, cars would drive by with people shouting "nigger" out the window while throwing eggs or rocks at me. I never understood why those people hated me so much when I'd done nothing except be born to my race. At eleven years old I was told, "Take your dirty black hands off my daughter!" on a playground.

As I became older, I noticed that the "good guys" in the movies wore white hats and the bad guys wore black hats. I saw that Superman, Batman, Spiderman, Santa Claus, and even Jesus himself did not resemble people of my race. Whenever it came to any would be role model, they would always be taken down in some form of disgrace or shame. For example, Martin Luther King was reportedly a plagiarist and an adulterer, Michael Jackson was a child molester, OJ Simpson is a murderer, James Brown was a wife beater, Mike Tyson is a rapist...and I can go on and on.

Realizing that it is against the unspoken American rule that black men cannot be glorified, all one has to do is notice the pictures of the faces on ALL OF THE MONEY. There are songs that refer to it as the "Almighty Dollar."

Because of the inescapable race problem, I became determined to outsmart the corrupt system. I found the most success as an entrepreneur whenever people did not know that there was a black man behind it. I hired white people as employees and remained invisible and my business thrived every time. As soon as anyone of any race discovered I was black, there was always an immediate assumption that there is the existence of something wrong or defective somewhere in my business because of it. I know now that this is mainly due to the stereotypical depiction of us because, as I've seen throughout my entire life, it is always the worst of us who get all of the airtime. If you are a black person willing to disgrace your race, the media will elevate you to stardom.

Gangster rap, hip hop, pants worn halfway around the ass, and the most vulgar lyrics and images of blacks...now that fits the depiction narrative . In fact, I notice that no matter what level of greatness I achieve, the news media is not interested, but if I go out and commit a crime, the media will make me a superstar overnight.

I finally ended up in jail twice for crimes I never did. I gave up and turned to drugs and alcohol. I deeply hated myself and wanted to die because I lost all hope upon realizing just how corrupt and unfair the world seemed to me at the time.

In September of 2004 I was sleeping on my friend's couch at his house sitting while he was away for the weekend. I drank nothing but vodka the entire time on an empty stomach. I would wake up and drink myself back to sleep. On the third day I could feel myself dying -literally. I could feel my soul departing from my body and in that moment, I stopped and said to God, "If I clean up my life from here forward, what will you do?"

Well, I did not get an immediate answer, but I quit smoking and drinking and started working out and fasting. Initially it was extremely rough because I was an addict going through detoxification. Every atom and cell in my being was begging me to come back, but I became angry at the drugs for doing that to me and I never returned. I felt that anything that would cause me all of that agony while trying to quit was definitely not worth starting again.

I now realize that blaming and excuses are the recipe that losers use to fail and that persistence and determination are mandatory to succeed.

The birth of the internet was the biggest game changer for me as a black businessman because I can do business with the entire world now without my race being visible and without my criminal history as eternal condemnation to all who judge others that way.

As I continued to get cleaner and cleaner in my lifestyle, I noticed that the human race is suffering from every ailment and disease that we can create a name for because of our ignorant neglect of internal cleansing. We take showers and baths, cars to the car wash, and clothes to the cleaners, but none of this cleans us on the inside. When I learned that Mahatma Gandhi said, "Be the change you want to see in the world", this became my creed and marching orders.

I also learned that the "symptoms of aging" are nothing but the accumulation of filth within a body temple that never cleanses. Since May of 2012 I have fasted (no food – water only) for the first seven days of every month. Today at the time of this writing I have fasted 400 days over fifty-six consecutive months but remember, the American culture in general cannot glorify a black man no matter what the achievement. Since fasting is the most feared and most misunderstood cure of nearly all ailments and diseases, I produced a short video series on YouTube that goes into greater detail entitled "The Cause and Cure of Human Suffering".

Always remember, Cleanliness is next to Godliness – internally – externally – eternally. The first Law of Nature is "Purification of Path." This is why it rains, why the winds blow, and why the rivers run. It is also why we catch colds: because Mother Nature is constantly cleaning so that more and more truth and light can emerge.

As far as God's answer to my question, today I am the CEO at ThePower.com, the Executive Director at ThePower.org, and the inventor of the revolutionary and absolutely amazing Personal Time-Map System. I am also a syndicated newspaper columnist who writes the Empowerment Column every week for the Las Vegas Informer and I write the inspirational Mars vs. Venus section in the prestigious Las Vegas Woman magazine as the only male ever allowed in this all-woman publication. I am the author of several books, including All About You and The Secret Wisdom of the Ages. Today I am known as the world's foremost authority in the scriptural and scientific teachings rediscovered in the ancient science of the standard deck of fifty-two playing cards.

During my years in college I majored in Physics and minored in Comparative Religions. I majored in physics because my deepest passion is to fix things, but before one can fix anything, one must first understand how it works or operates and physics explains how the universe works and explains it mathematically. I studied comparative religions because I was always fascinated by the powerful influential effect religion has on its followers.

While studying religion and noticing how they all differ, I became even more interested in figuring out the common denominator, or where they all agreed. What kept coming up for me was the word "Truth." The Bhagavad Gita says, "The Truth is triumphant and always prevails in the end." The Holy Quran says, "The Truth is eternal and everlasting." And the Holy Bible says, "The Truth shall set you free."

At that point I realized that it was not religion that I sought. But I wanted to know where one could find this Truth they were all pointing in the direction of? So I became a self-proclaimed "Truth Seeker". During a high stakes poker game (well, it was high stakes according to my wallet) upon losing all of my chips, I watched the winner raking the big pile to himself while saying, "Well, the cards don't lie." Now as a Truth Seeker who has studied the great religions of the world, this was the stone left unturned.

Upon investigation, I learned things about the deck of cards that nothing else in existence can claim. For example, no matter where we are in the world, if we walk into a casino, we will see that they are all in agreement around ONE DECK only! It is not Tarot cards or Angel cards, but it is the standard deck of playing cards that attracts all of the money.

The deck of fifty-two playing cards also is the only scripture in existence that remains unrevised since its origin and there still exists no authority in the world that can change the structure of the deck. For example, the king of any country cannot order the removal of the Six of Diamonds because he doesn't like the card. The Bible has over a thousand versions, e.g. the Catholic version, the Jehovah's Witness version, the Book of Mormon or King James version, etc.

When I discovered that the fifty-two cards actually represent the fifty-two weeks in the year and the twelve Royal cards (Jacks, Queens, Kings) represent the twelve months and the twelve a.m. and twelve p.m. hours in the day, the student of Einstein as physics major kicked in and I invented the Personal Time-Map System. I teach that the real name of the game is not Poker or Blackjack, but it is to succeed in the four suits.

Success is available to anyone willing to do whatever it takes to overcome the challenges that most often get in the way of any worthwhile achievement. Applying enough persistence and determination is the key to conquering any challenge. Simply stated, if we do the things that make people succeed, we will succeed, and if we do the things that make people fail, we will fail.

Total Success is divided into 4 areas:

1. Emotional ♥ Success

2. Mental ♣ Success

3. Financial ♦ Success

4. Spiritual ♠ Success

Emotional Success is achieving mastery in unconditional love and happiness. Emotional Success is revealed through our family and friend relationships. Emotional Success is a complete and total forgiveness and acceptance of yourself and/or anybody else needing forgiveness. Emotional Success is the compassion to realize that no one is defective and that everyone is doing their best within their circumstance, beliefs and education.

Mental Success is achieving mastery in Knowhow, Intelligence and Intuition. Mental Success is the realization that life has an unerring way of putting us in the perfect situations and circumstances necessary for our growth and development into higher states of consciousness. Mental Success causes the revelation that life is our greatest teacher, always sending feedback messages. For example, if we don't like the results, life is telling us that we need to change how we are going about it. For this reason, there is no such thing as failure; only feedback.

Financial Success is achieving Abundance and Prosperity consciousness. Prosperity and Abundance consciousness is the realization that scarcity, lack, and limitations are only self-created illusions. Our truthful reality is, we have more air than we can breathe, more water than we can drink, more people than we can meet, and more places than we can go. Financial Success is a realization that it's not the money that we really want, but the things that money can buy. Long-lasting Financial Success results from impeccable integrity in all business dealings. Two important things to remember for achieving Financial Success are:

1. Keep it Simple

2. Money is Attracted to Good Ideas

Spiritual Success is achieving Perfect Health, Higher States of Consciousness, and Divine Wisdom. Spiritual Success is our Soul becoming awake into the unbounded power, infinite and eternal nature of the "I Am Presence". Spiritual Success turns our problems into an opportunity to reveal our level of consciousness. Proper nutrition and exercise, cleansing, and purification are the way to Spiritual Success. Practicing daily meditation in addition to proper sleep accelerates the process of attaining Spiritual Success. Divine Wisdom is the realization that "We cannot control everything, but we can control our response to anything" and how we respond to things that happen reveals our level of maturity and Spiritual Success.

Right action will advance us closer to or even beyond our goals. www.ThePower.org offers a proven, scientific system that provides you with the power of illuminating Light to help guide you into making the right decisions

Eternal Blessings ♥ ♣ ♦ ♠

## *MEET REVEREND THABITI...*

Reverend Thabiti is the CEO at ThePower.com, Executive Director at ThePower.org, and is best known as the inventor of the world's first Personal Time-Map System which is an interactive birth chart (exclusively provided at ThePower.org) that integrates ANY birth date with universal laws governing existence as structured in the rediscovered ancient science of the standard deck of 52 playing cards.

He is the author of several books, including, *All About You* and *The Secret Wisdom of the Ages*. His book *All About You* answers the old proverb "Know Thyself." His book *The Secret Wisdom of the Ages* has a foreword written by Michael Bernard Beckwith, the Founder and Spiritual Director of the Agape International Spiritual Center in Los Angeles.

Reverend Thabiti also writes the nationally syndicated Empowerment Column every week in the *Las Vegas Informer* newspaper. He is featured in the movie documentary *The Illumined Ones*.

He is an international expert on the subject of fasting and says that the human race is suffering from every ailment and disease that we can create a name for because of our ignorant neglect of the vital importance of internal cleansing through fasting and diet. He also says that illness is our body's natural response to what we are doing wrong.

Reverend Thabiti is considered by thousands as the world's foremost authority in the scriptural and scientific teachings rediscovered in the ancient science of the standard deck of 52 playing cards.

## *Contact Information for Reverend Thabiti:*

Direct:     (720) 987-5252

Email:      CEO@ThePower.com

Website:   www.ThePower.com

## BREAKING BARRIERS TO BECOME A CHAMPION
### By Coach Sherry Winn

Imagine if you lost your "self," the one characteristic that made you who you are—that defined you. What would you do? Would you get up, dust yourself off, pull up your big girl panties (or tighty-whities), and have faith that you would find yourself again? Would you be able to break through the barriers that were preventing you from connecting with your inner winner? Or would you be like most people: devastated, heartbroken, and fearful that you would never be YOU again? The story I'm about to share with you is a story about how I lost myself, and how my five-year journey changed EVERYTHING I believed.

In the summer of 1996, I departed my position as the head women's basketball coach at Montana State University-Northern to seek new challenges. After winning 139 games and a national championship, I believed I needed tougher situations, so I could grow as a person and a coach.

I regretted asking for tougher challenges during the next five years thousands of times. Not only did I regret asking, but I begged the universe to cancel my words, mark through them, toss them aside, and pretend I had never spoken them.

Two months after departing MSU-Northern, I developed intense pain in my back and right leg. I don't know how to explain this pain to you; I couldn't define the pain to the seventeen medical professionals who examined me. How do you define an intense pain that appears from nowhere and leaves you debilitated?

The first doctor examined me and proclaimed that I was suffering from the maladies of getting older. I was only thirty-three! Granted, I'd pushed my body farther than most people, training twice a day for twelve years in preparation for the 1984 and 1988 Olympics, where I competed in team handball, a sport is that like soccer without the hands or water polo on land. I departed the first doctor's office angry and disappointed, but with absolute faith that another medical professional would possess the answer.

Two years later after seeking help from orthopedists, acupuncturists, chiropractors, massage therapists, and neurologists, the only help I had was a name to my disorder: chronic pain. I discovered that even doctors have limitations when it comes to knowledge about human bodies.

If you've experienced a broken limb and felt the nauseating pain after the first few minutes of shock, then you understand what I felt daily. Imagine if you couldn't walk through a grocery store long enough to buy groceries, or sit in a movie theater long enough to watch a movie. Even though I was an Olympic athlete and pain was nothing new to me, chronic pain was beyond my pain threshold. During my athletic life, I played with sprained ankles, sore knees, bruised thighs, a broken nose, fingers, and a big toe, but chronic pain robbed me of doing what I loved the most: being an athlete.

What do you do when the medical professionals tell you that they don't have an answer? You've done everything in your power and everything the specialists have told you, but you've fallen short of your goals. The barrier in front of you is too high, too wide, and too thick.

I don't know what you would do, but what I did was get angry, discouraged, and desperate. After two years without answers, my desperation sunk into depression. Something had to change. Either I got better, or I found a way to end the misery by terminating me.

Thoughts of suicide became my normal. First the thoughts were a whisper, barely heard above the din of the constant pain, and then as the pain lingered, month after month with no hope of a cure, the thoughts bombarded me. I fought the suicidal thoughts with the tools I knew—anger and determination, but as my hope dwindled, I welcomed life-ending ideas as my answer to salvation.

The seventeenth medical professional who examined me said, "I'll get a team of doctors together. We will review all your X-rays, CAT scans, bone scans, and tests. We will come up with a game plan for you."

A week later, hopeful of a positive outcome, I returned to the doctor. The doctor said, "We've reviewed all your information and think that your best course of action is to go to a pain management clinic." I jumped up and ran for the door. The doctor asked, "Where are you going?"

I stopped, turned, and glared at him. "I don't want to learn to manage the pain. I want to get RID of the pain."

That was the last doctor I saw.

My message to you is not that medical professionals are inept; my message is that sometimes you may have to seek alternative answers that are not in your comfort zone. Sometimes you must go beyond what the experts know.

Although I thought of giving up and giving in, raising the white flag of surrender, and taking enough pain pills to make certain I never had any pain again, my years of training for the Olympics kicked in. You cannot be an Olympian and quit at every barrier that gets in your way.

I searched for different answers. I read books and asked questions. I prayed to a God I had forgotten.

When hope seemed a distant dream and my motivation to live was shriveling, I met an angel. She didn't have wings, a halo, or a white robe, but I knew she was an angel.

Do you believe in angels? I didn't until I met one.

The next day after I was informed that pain management was my option, inspiration draining out of me, hopelessness pervading me, I barely found the strength to roll out of bed. After getting dressed, I drove my Volkswagen Jetta to the University of Southern Colorado where I pretended to coach my basketball team. I didn't do any coaching; I spent my time fighting the pain rolling on me like tidal waves, and the anger covering me like a flock of crows. My coaching record reflected my misery, the team barely winning a game for two years, fighting amongst themselves, and blaming each other for our losses.

On the day that the angel entered my life, I was on the way to work, stopping at United Bank to cash a check. I stared at the doors to the bank and could not believe the distance of ten yards was too far for me to conquer. A white van pulled in next to me, and I grabbed my car door, pulling it closed allowing the driver to park. The doors opened, and a stump of a woman emerged. With her torso and short leg stumps, she stood three feet tall.

From my car seat, I watched as she "walked" to the bank doors by thrusting her arms out in front of her, and then swinging her torso forward through her arms. She propelled herself through the parking lot in seven seconds. When she reached the door, she hopped on her stumps to grab the door handle. With the door handle in her hand, she leaned back, swung the door open, released the handle, and scooted her way into the building.

Peeling off my self-pity like a snake skin that had lingered too long, I followed her into the bank, mesmerized by her determination.

She torso swung into a chair by placing her hands on the seat and heaving herself onto the chair. In midair, she performed a 180 degree turn so that she could face the lobby. Once seated, she lasered her brown eyes directly at mine.

I walked toward my hero who had pulled a checkbook out of her purse and was writing on a deposit slip. When I got within five feet of her, I stopped and walked back toward the bank teller.

Gaining courage, I pivoted again and walked to her. I said, "I'm sorry. I don't mean to interrupt you or stare at you. I just wanted to tell you that you are an inspiration. I don't know how you do what you do daily. I have chronic pain and I...well...I...am angry every day. And today, you helped me."

She smiled. "Thank you."

"Do you mind if I ask you a question?"

She leaned back in the chair, causing her stumps to lift four inches off the seat. "No, go ahead."

"You don't seem to be mad. If I were you, I'd be furious, really pissed off. Angry at the world and ready to kill anybody who was in my path, yet you seem almost serene. How do you do it?"

She rocked herself to lean forward on the chair. "I was mad and angry and pissed at the world for three years and you know what it got me?"

"No. What?"

"More anger. Nobody wants to be around a legless, angry woman. My husband left me, my friends deserted me, my family ran from me, and it wasn't because of the loss of my legs. It was because of my anger. After I lost everything, I decided I couldn't get my legs back, but I could get my joy back. And so, I did."

What I learned from my angel was that <u>pity didn't serve me well</u>.

By fixating my thoughts on doom and gloom, I saw and felt more of the same. One thing was certain: *feeling sorry for myself didn't make my circumstances better. Swimming around in self-pity only made me feel worse.*

Nothing physical changed for me that day. The pain didn't magically disappear, nor did I slide away from suicidal thoughts. What did happen was that a small opening occurred in my thoughts, and this is how huge changes begin—by one small thought.

If you can shift one thought - just move six inches over from where you're at - you allow yourself the opportunity for bigger shifts to happen. After seeing my angel, I understood one powerful statement: **being negative about my situation made me worse**.

How did I get better? The journey was long. I read self-help books, practiced positive thinking, and meditated. I searched other means for healing, and repeatedly told myself that there was an answer to my pain, even if the doctors didn't know what it was.

After two years of enduring the pain, searching for answers wherever I went, I purchased a book called *The Egoscue Method,* reading the entire book in a day. The following day I called the Egoscue Clinic in California and flew to San Diego to meet with their therapists.

My pain intensity was reduced from a ten to a six after a single two-hour session with the Egoscue therapists. For the first time in sixteen months, I walked for thirty minutes without pain.

The therapists at the clinic developed a series of daily exercises for me, which took an hour and half to finish, but after completion of the exercises, I functioned at a higher level. I wasn't healed, but I could walk and sit without intense pain.

For five years, I continued to perform the Egoscue exercises. While the exercises allowed me to function at a higher level, the pain was excruciating by the time I headed to bed in the evenings. Even though I diligently exercised, only missing fourteen days in five years, I depended on the exercises to negate my pain, and sometimes, when the exercises failed me, I would sink back into massive pain.

You might think after reading the last few paragraphs that you wouldn't have exercised for an hour and a half every day, so you could walk. But pain is a great motivator, isn't it?

Pain is your wake-up call. Pain signals you to pay attention, to look at life a little bit differently, to make shifts, listen to your higher self, get out of your anger, let go of the past, and forgive. *Pain is a messenger*. Maybe you don't like your pain message. I didn't like my messages either. But eventually, I understood what I needed so desperately to hear.

Because I was managing the pain and not healing the pain, I searched for something else.

In 2001, Lori, a friend who saw me in pain every day for the past five years, tried to help by offering a different solution. "Sherry, why don't you try Integrative Manual Therapy? It is a therapy that works on the body, mind, and spirit."

"I've worked on my spirits - drank every type of booze there is and still woke up in pain - with the addition of a headache. I've seen specialists, chiropractors, physical therapists, acupuncturists, massage therapists, and even a psychic. Get this.

The psychic told me in a past life regression that I was a decorated general, and led thousands of soldiers into a massacre. *THAT thought made me feel a WHOLE lot better!"*

Lori said, "Sherry, what do you have to lose by trying something else?"

"My money. My hope. My sanity. Nothing much."

But at that point in my life, I was so desperate that I was cruising the pharmacy aisles searching for snake oil. Heck, I would have rubbed snake oil between my eyelashes if it would have make a difference.

I made an appointment with the Integrative Manual Therapist. If you had walked into that office, after you had paused to smell the burning sage, you would have heard the meditation music playing softly in the background, and you would have been as startled as I was by the sight of my female therapist, Carol, who had just returned from a spiritual trip to Peru, walking into the room sporting a freshly shaven head. Yeah, I wanted to walk out too, but I needed the snake oil.

I stared at Carol's bald head as she said, "Sherry, I want you to think about some of the emotions you've bottled up since age thirteen."

Cranking up five years of loaded sarcasm, I asked, "What? Are you out of snake oil?"

Carol, undaunted by my hostility, said, "Let me ask you a question, Sherry. How many doctors have you seen and how many tests have they run on you?"

I knew this answer. I'd been telling anybody who would listen about my horrific pain for five years. "Around seventeen doctors, and I've had all the tests: bone scans, CAT scans, MRI's, X-rays, all of them."

Carol allowed silence to linger between us before she asked, "How has that worked out for you?"

I said, "I know forty-seven physical ailments that I don't have."

"Then let's look at some of the emotional pain that is crippling you."

I got up and walked out of the room. Why was Carol asking me about emotional pain? Couldn't see she that I was suffering from physical pain? This whole idea about the body, mind, and spirit being connected was just downright idiotic. I needed somebody who understood my pain, not some bald, Buddha-minded teacher.

Departing from Carol's office, my stomach tightened, causing a nauseating feeling. Since I suffered from hypoglycemia, and when I didn't eat every couple of hours, I got light-headed, angry, frustrated, and nauseous, I believed food would resolve the issue.

Sitting down at a restaurant with a friend, Lynne, I shoveled chicken and Brussel sprouts down my throat, attempting to ease my symptoms. When the pain intensified, I doubled over, holding my stomach. Wobbling to the bathroom, I prayed for a release to the pain. After five minutes in the bathroom without relief, I made my way back to Lynne.

Lynne said, "I think you need to go back to the clinic."

"Why? So I can snort sage and shave my head?" I hesitated for moment and then added, "And do you know what that therapist wants me to do - she wants me to talk...about E-M-O-T-I-O-N-S!"

Lynne called Carol and we drove back to the clinic. When I opened the door, and walked in, Carol took one look at me and smiled knowingly. "Are you ready to deal with the emotions you've been battling for the past twenty-five years or do you want to stay in pain? Your choice."

*How desperate for answers do you have to be before you open your mind to new ways of breaking old barriers?*

I was that desperate. Have you ever been that desperate?

I asked, "Carol, what do you want me to do?"

She inhaled a yogic breath and answered, "Can you think of one person right now who you hurt you so badly that you can't forgive her?"

"One? I can think of a dozen. Give me a couple of minutes and I can think of fifty."

Carol chuckled at my humorous attempt and asked, "Who is the one person that you absolutely cannot forgive—the one who has hurt you the most?"

Closing my eyes, I felt the answer, but I wasn't certain I could say it aloud. Vulnerability was not my strength. I mumbled, "Me. It's me."

Five minutes later, I slid off the table free of stomach pain. Carol didn't heal my chronic pain that day, but what she did was open my mind to the possibility that holding onto the past—to the anger, grief, blame, guilt, and betrayal I felt was hurting me. There was a connection between the physical pain, and my unwillingness to let go of the past.

What past events held their death grip on me?

Nothing outrageous. Probably nothing you haven't experienced. I felt betrayed, abandoned, hated, ostracized, unloved, and despised. I had a mother who loved me, but who abandoned me during her life crisis, teammates who cheered against me and wanted me removed from the team, a coach who sexually harassed me, a partner who had an affair. Nothing so vile that I couldn't have recovered from the events, but I chose to repeat those stories and hold them as evidence that life was brutally unfair.

I can't prove to you that forgiveness assisted me in healing, that forgiveness was what ended my chronic pain of five years, or that forgiveness is what allowed me to break through my barriers. I can tell you that I never took a drug or had a surgery. I can tell you that I've spent hundreds of hours working on forgiving other people and forgiving myself. I can tell you that I'm a better person, that I'm not as angry, that I'm more understanding and loving. AND I can tell you that while I'm not 100% healthy, I've hiked, biked, walked, weight trained, and played basketball.

I can also tell you this: you can't just pay lip service to forgiveness. Forgiveness must be real. How do you move to real forgiveness? I'd like to share with you the three most powerful techniques that worked for me.

1. Believe your ultimate journey is not to have or do, but to become the best person you can become by growing through your life lessons. My life lesson wasn't to become an Olympian, but to become more loving and compassionate.

2. When you feel like somebody else is doing something to you, ask what are they doing FOR you? Not to you, but for you. How is the person giving you an opportunity to evolve?

3. Take responsibility for your feelings and reactions. Know by changing the way you feel about events, people, and

circumstances that you can change the events, people, or circumstances.

Embracing the past allows you to be free of your barriers. When you hold onto the pain and retell your story, you keep the pain in you. Breaking the barriers to your past is a challenge. You might believe that holding onto painful memories keeps you safe, that if you let those memories go, the other person gets away with hurting you. Those are stories you tell yourself, but they are not true stories.

Whatever your dreams are, whatever barriers are preventing you from success, you can overcome them. I've been helping people break their barriers for twenty-seven years. When I understood that the number one challenge for my players was not learning the game of basketball but overcoming their self-imposed limitations, I developed a system for helping them. That same system can be applied to you. Whether you are an athlete, a life insurance salesperson, or an entrepreneur, you have a winner within you that is waiting to be unleashed. If you want to learn more about how you can use your barriers as a means for success, contact me at coachwinn@coachwinnspeaks.com or view my website at www.coachwinnspeaks.com.

## MEET COACH SHERRY WINN...

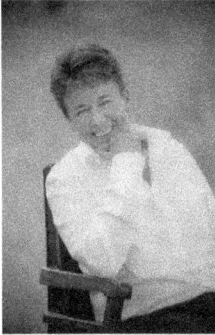

Coach Sherry Winn is an in-demand motivational speaker, a leading success coach and seminar trainer, a two-time Olympian, a national championship basketball coach, and an Amazon bestseller. She has written five books, including *Unleash the Winner within You: A Success Game Plan for Business, Leadership and Life*. Thousands of people, from small business owners to athletic coaches to corporate executives, have enjoyed Coach Winn's powerful, interactive, and humorous WINNING presentations.

With over thirty-four years of practicing leadership as an elite athlete and collegiate basketball coach, Sherry is an expert on coaching leaders and team members to championship status. She has successfully taken people beyond their levels of comfort to "WIN" against competitors who were superior in talent, facilities, and financial budgets. Through her WIN Philosophy™ and WINNER Principles™, she teaches leaders and team members to be victorious even when the odds appear to be insurmountable.

A recognized authority on leadership and team development, Coach Winn shares with you the WINNER Principles which will enable you to rejuvenate, invigorate, and stimulate you and your team members to become agents of change.

Audiences rave about Coach Winn's ability to enthusiastically deliver messages woven into humorous stories, which are applicable for individuals within all levels of organizations. A passionate, sought-after author, speaker, and business consultant, Coach Winn is characterized by friends, colleagues, and clients as one of the most benevolent, perceptive, and influential individuals in the business today.

Coach Winn is the originator of the WIN Philosophy ™ and the WINNER Principles™ and is known for her passion and belief system that ALL things are possible.

### *Contact Information for Coach Cherry Winn:*

Telephone:     304-380-4398
Email:         coachwinn@coachwinnspeaks.com
Website:       www.coachwinnspeaks.com.
Facebook
 & Twitter:    coachwinnspeaks

# WILL ADVERSITY FORGE YOU INTO SOMETHING GREAT?
### By Jo Anna Wright

I was running for my life on a dark country road, one month after a difficult knee surgery. Outside, children are playing in the streets under the moonlight which would soon witness my fight for survival. What they were about to see was a madman speeding down the road in a one-ton truck aimed directly at me. He had already fought off twelve of my friends to get to me and the host of the party we were attending found himself tossed like a ragdoll onto his cement driveway. I knew my only hope was to somehow escape with my life.

For most of my existence I had been a strong woman, both mentally and financially, so I felt I could accomplish anything I put my mind to without hesitation. I had my hand in drag racing, acquired a ton of knowledge about motors and used it, went on many excursions on my motorcycle, and mastered the art of single parenting. Other women even looked up to me as a role model. So, I finally asked the question, "What happened to the woman I had grown to admire & respect?" How could I have slipped into this abyss of fear and doubt?

The answer was not only quite clear but was most certainly the same answer echoed by women who had, like me, relinquished their power to another. I was no longer in control of my own life. My partner was hateful and violent toward everyone, especially me. The years of physical and mental abuse had taken their toll and stripped me of everything, including my pride. I had no car, no phone, and no money. Crying didn't seem to ease the pain of feeling stuck and afraid. Even my son, who is now an adult, wanted to know what had happened to his mom. I knew that very night that I had to get away from this toxic situation and it would take all the courage I could muster to do it. I guess my guardian angel was watching over me, seeing as I am still here.

Fortunately, I finally was able to find a safe haven from the madman's pursuit.. With the help of trusted friends and a safe place to stay, I was able to leave that unhealthy relationship and start building the new me. It was then that I began to reflect on growing up in a dysfunctional family and the impact it had on my life as an adult. Maybe there were clues to my temporary departure from who I thought I was deep inside.

My mother was a Type 1 a diabetic since the age of ten and nearly died giving birth to my sister and myself. She knew she wasn't supposed to bear children, as the risk was great. Having two daughters was a double blow as she only wanted to have sons, so she resented us even more. My sister got more beatings from her than I did simply because she was the spitting image of our mother, who hated herself.

My dad, on the other hand, took everything out on me. My sister and I got it from different directions, but we endured the hardships and became stronger because of it. We both swore and promised that we would never raise our children the way we were raised.

I grew up in Union City, California. Even though my dad was abusive to me, I was my father's favorite "son". I took to cars and wrenching on engines like a duck to water. I knew every tool he used by the age of ten, was driving by twelve, and started drag racing the quarter mile at fifteen. I loved the race track and that father/daughter connection. I was well on my way as a drag racer, winning trophies and making my dad proud. It was also my path to confidence as an adult.

In my younger days, my dad was a welder and he would take me with him on jobs, welding eighteen-wheel trucks that broke down on the road. Those eighteen-wheel trucks were a passion of mine since the age of five. Eventually it would be my dream to drive across the United States to see the country. I took diesel tech in high school, educated myself on the big Cummins engine, and, working as a team with my other classmates, I was key in putting one together from the ground up. No mechanic would ever be able to take advantage of this girl, since I could talk their language. Science became another passion of mine. I would often imagine how science could change the world. Maybe it could even change my life. I was always being creative and saying to myself, "Why not?" Yes, I was a Big Thinker, but all that changed when I became pregnant.

I was only sixteen and disowned by my parents. No more drag racing. I dropped out of diesel tech and life as I knew it was about to drastically change. Yet, in a strange and ironic way, I knew it was a blessing in disguise. Against my parents' wishes, I had my son. He is now twenty-nine and is the best child a mother could ask for. When my mother found out I was having a boy, her tune changed to one of pride and anticipation of having the son she had always wanted. All her friends came to the baby shower, but none of my friends were invited. She became increasingly possessive after my son was born. My mother hired detectives and lawyers to explore ways to have him taken from me. Her goal was to declare me an unfit mother.

The day I moved out was quite memorable. She said, "You can't take our son away from us", as if she had any right to claim him for her own. Her obsession may have contributed to her declining health from the diabetes, so she eventually gave up the fight. At the age of eight, my son was a pallbearer at her funeral. RIP, Mother.

Now it was just the two of us because my son's father never expressed any interest in having a relationship with him. There were no shared custody issues and no grandmother trying to take him away from me anymore. That sense of relief was short-lived as new and challenging problems would take the place of those fears of the past, but we did the best we could despite those challenges. My son would learn to be confident with his skills and to ask questions to gain knowledge. That knowledge would help him become the confident and successful entrepreneur he is today.

He announced to me just recently, "The older I get, the easier I can see how hard it must have been to have a kid so young." He has always been my rock and my compass, even though I strayed from my course on occasion. He has run his own business since the age of eighteen and has traveled the nation. It takes a lot of tenacity to be an entrepreneur, but it's even more remarkable that he has been that way since day one. I will always be proud of the adult he has become. He is now engaged to his beautiful fiancée and living in San Diego.

I became an entrepreneur in 2000 at the age of thirty. I had not yet mastered those skills, but for the time being I would be satisfied with "winging it" in real estate. I started out in the lending industry as a mortgage broker, then as a real estate investor, and eventually I became a real estate agent to excel in my investments. Once I realized all the creative things you could do with real estate, I knew I had found my true calling. It brought out the "mad scientist" in me and became more intriguing with every day that passed.

I found the lending industry to be truly amazing. However, I was puzzled by the complicated transactions and how it all fit together at the time. As I started to digest the terms, work the numbers, and understand it all better, I graduated to loan officer in 2001. My skills expanded as I did some real estate investing for myself in Idaho. I saw many avenues you could take in real estate and I was determined to learn them all. Now, from those experiences, I am able to mix and match to create a successful result, whether for myself or a client. I now train on the "4 levels of real estate investing", which makes the perfect cocktail for anyone interested in real estate.

At the time of this writing, I am involved in multiple real estate deals, one of which is a $29,000,000 land development project in Maui. It's the biggest one in my life and very exciting. I also have students nationwide who are learning strategies in Wholesale, Fix and Flip, Buy and Hold and Money Lending (Lazy Assets). They are experiencing that same excitement through my webinars and workshops, not to mention the great returns on their investments. Just recently I received a multimillion dollar real estate award that makes me realize how amazing my life has become.

My life wasn't always so blessed as an adult. In 2008, like so many others, I lost everything. Flat broke and as I mentioned in the beginning, I was in a destructive relationship that almost led to my death, I spiraled down to the lowest point I could imagine. All my investments were gone. Poor choices coupled with being under the rule of a tyrant increased the magnitude of the losses I had suffered. I had never been so alone. When my own son saw me in this sad state, he wanted to know what happened to the strong mother he had grown up with. It forced me to do some serious soul searching to find that answer as well as what I was willing to do to change it. That was the turning point. I found the strength and money to leave the relationship, poured myself back into the industry that nearly destroyed me, and began to invest in myself with a vengeance. I surrounded myself with people that were interested in helping me become successful. I went to seminars and workshops and read books about self-development and every real estate course I could find. Slowly I started seeing the success I knew I deserved, but the change in me was nothing less than extraordinary.

Since that time, I have developed a community of people seeking the knowledge to become successful in real estate investing. My desire to help them avoid the mistakes I made is fueled by my passion for the industry, ensuring proper education and helping them develop the entrepreneur skills needed to achieve the success they seek. I have trained hundreds of people nationwide and building wealth with little or no money has become a reality for many of my students.

I was recently honored at a national convention, where I received a standing ovation and received an award named in my honor. The "Wright" award will be given to someone each year for their contributions in helping others succeed in the real estate industry. Since 2013 I have done $123,000,000 in real estate transactions, but the best part of what I do is to witness my students building their personal wealth using some of the creative strategies learned through their education with me.

Another great chapter of my life involved meeting the man of my dreams. He treats me like a queen and it's remarkable how we share so many similar desires and finish each other's sentences. He has the patience for my entrepreneurial world with unlimited support and the connection we have is strong, yet flexible. We have so much fun together that I barely remember the life I had before we met.

What I've learned most about life is that misfortune will always rear its ugly head, but self- development is a never-ending process. In spite of your upbringing, you can and must succeed to your better self that awaits. What really matters is to have faith in yourself and the process. Your parents are NOT the problem, only the teachers of what you are put on this earth to learn and helps others with.

So I guess it comes down to the question, "Will adversity forge you into something great?" The choice is yours. I would love to connect with you

I am Jo Anna Wright...a survivor, a teacher, and focused woman

## *MEET JO ANNA WRIGHT...*

Jo Anna is personally recognized as an expert creating more than $5 million in real estate transactions for her students changing the lives of hundreds nationwide with her step-by-step "Bottom line Wealth" strategies. She has over 17 years of experience in real estate as a licensed professional, Investor and Entrepreneur Strategist. Teaching people how to build wealth and keep more of the money they make with tax strategies and real estate assets.

She has personally been mentored by Sharon Lechter, the co-founder of the Rich Dad Poor Dad curriculum, 7- figure real estate investing instructors along with Zig Ziglar, Brian Tracy, Jim Rohn, Les Brown, and many other leaders within the industry.

Her vision of making a global impact on 1 million women entrepreneurs attaining financial independence while loving their sexy assets. Jo Anna offers an uplifting, collaborative, and educational environment. Providing concrete solutions, realistic goals and a customized road map. This keeps her grounded in her purpose to help women rise!

She is an award-winning mentor, investor and national speaker.

## Contact Information for Jo Anna Wright:

Direct:         209-346-1014
Email: *joanna@joannawright.net*

# ABOUT THE COMPILER AND THE MINDSET
# BEHIND THE BOOK

As I sit alone in my five-bedroom house earlier filled with the laughter of friends, and memories of my family, it is quiet now, and I start to write down the beginning of a song that would serve as a theme song for an organization in 2014. The song would be about *being a part of something grander*, being a *"beacon of hope"* for those in need of hope those that are thinking about giving up. The real theme of the song is about the continual healing we all go through in life and our responsibility to help others as we get help. The song resonates with the chorus urging people to look around and consider the people that are hurting and to take an active part of helping others that are fighting through their battles in life and to give them some hope. It emphasizes how we are all "Healings In Motion". The words seemed to flow so easily for me when I was writing it...almost effortlessly for a song that carries this much significance, depth, and meaning.

Fast forward to the present day, the song has been heard by thousands of people at various events and over the radio to help inspire people. As I reflect back, it is literally four years and three months ago (as I write this chapter) since I wrote the song, which still serves as a positive trigger device to help me remember the feeling I had that prompted the words to the song. The song is so significant for me because of the memories and life experiences it represents for me. It also reminds me why I do what I do and to never give up on people or myself.

During the time I wrote the song, I was starting the process of separation in my marriage. It was a defining moment that was the culmination of the two prior years that had led to the beginning of the end of my marriage. If you have experienced a loss, someone described divorce as a death only you are reminded about the person every time you see them, especially if kids are involved. I had always believed that marriage was forever and the timeless promise of the beautiful vow "...to have and to hold, for better or worse, for richer or poorer, in sickness and in health, till death do us part". Unfortunately, the person that I had been married to for over twenty years did not feel the same way based on her decision and would decide to make the decision to end the marriage. I never thought this would be a real possibility as I never believed in divorce and it wasn't ever a real option for me. So I was taken aback when she actually decided to take action on it.

As a couple, we were always a great team together...helping others, always serving in our community...but clearly, the result shows that we did not spend enough time to ensure we were doing okay and somehow lost our way. It was so hard for me to understand why she would even head in that direction as we both knew the casualty that divorce leaves behind. I would immediately not just understand but readily personal experience why the process of divorce is so devastating. There was no physical abuse in our marriage or infidelity, so was completely side swiped by this possibility. "I am doing my best...THIS CAN'T BE HAPPENING TO ME."

At that time, being alone in the five bedroom home we had spent most of our time building our family memories in would be the same home that I would as now be alone in as I wrote the song reflecting about what I needed...help, guidance, and a true sense of hope and healing myself. The completion of the song and having it professionally recorded and shared helped me translate my true feelings through music bringing a message that would serve others...knowing that it could affect thousands and possibly even hundreds of thousands of people over time is an inspiring thought. In an interesting way, completing the song helps keep me focused on my life's mission and every time I hear it played, the song helps also inspire me and brings me closer to some very important issues in my own life.

I honestly didn't realize all the emotional repercussions the process of divorce would have but have learned to embrace the lessons learned which helps ease the pain. What I realized was the importance of a few critical decisions I needed to make:

**DECISION 1:**    Never lose faith in God.

**DECISION 2:**    Forgive others, but even more importantly, FORGIVE YOURSELF.

**DECISION 3:**    Hold on tight to your dreams and make them a reality.

**DECISION 4:**    Don't Stop Believing in YOURSELF or others.

**DECISION 5:**    Make sure you take care of yourself first before others.

*"I think it's safe to say that most of you know a lot about my life whether I liked it or not, and I had to stop because I had everything and I was absolutely broken inside. And I kept it all together to where I never let you know. But, I kept it too much together where I let myself down."* ~Selena Gomez at the AMA

## GOOD DECISIONS: THE DIFFERENCE BETWEEN BEING THE DIFFERENCE OR BEING THE LESSON

I am now able to look at life from a fuller spectrum from my life's lessons and challenges. I look at things with a much deeper awareness as to what is happening in the world. Sometimes I will take time to observe people whether it be at a coffee shop or in a park. It's very interesting to think about what makes people different. I have seen a mother with a new born child, a couple clearly walking together but somewhat detached, and a professional business man ordering their coffee. I often wonder what is the story behind the person.

Many people go about life somewhat haphazardly while others seem overly regimented. Regardless, until we know the story of a person, I find it serves me to always show understanding, compassion, and grace where it is called for. Nevertheless, I know that no matter where we are at in life today, there are some exceptions to the rule, but for the most part, where we are at is probably a direct result of decisions we have made...even if our decision is indecision.

What makes a child that was raised in the projects able to rise above it all and become a Supreme Court Justice like Clarence Thomas while on the other hand a child that is raised in a wealthy family end up doing drugs and in prison? Many would absolutely agree that PASSION is key. However, it is the DECISIONS that passion drives us to make that can be pointed to for someone's success. Passion can be a double-edged sword, since on one hand it helps propel us to take risks and do some incredible things we normally wouldn't, and it drives us to get things done; while on the other hand, it can keep us committed to a path that may not serve us at that time if we don't make the right decisions.

*The ability to make "Good Decisions" is arguably one of the most important skills we can learn, which often requires emotional discipline and patience.*

We have probably heard the statement, *"We all have 24 hours in a day to work with",* implying everyone has the same amount of time and how we use it will determine our outcome in life. *Life will deal us challenges, and it is the challenging circumstances that help our passion and character grow and is where our real stories lie.* The struggles we endure and overcome help strengthen us and prepare us to do great things. Granted that many of our circumstances are different, but regardless, if we can make good decisions through even the difficult times, we are building our character and foundation to equip us for what we are called to accomplish in this lifetime. PASSION simply helps us get there faster.

Passion is sometimes analogous to fire. It can be the spark that ignites us to do incredible things. Our passion will drive us to make decisions to create the foundation and will serve us well if we are able to make consistently *"good decisions"*. On the other hand, if we make hasty decisions, we may find ourselves needing to spend much time and expense correcting a situation that rash decisions create. The importance of *"good decisions"* cannot be underestimated.

Here is to your life's journey and the good decisions you have made and will continue to make to fulfill your life's purpose. Enjoy the wonderful stories from the incredible authors of this book.

Currently, I serve on the Executive Board of Several established organization and businesses. I served as a Master Emcee for a variety of major events representing various multicultural, non-profit, and business communities. I also am a radio personality on MONEY 1055FM on Rush Hour For Success as the "Wok Star" and also have a daily segment "Wok The Talk" on The Voice Of Stockton-KXVS Radio which is the Community Radio Station for Stockton City. I have enjoyed serving a wide array of different types of people, cultures, and communities which gives me a very expansive perspective on different subjects. This book is designed to help inspire you through the stories of different people that have made significant decisions that have helped position them with the life experience and credibility to deliver a powerful message through the story of their life.

As I think about the many life experiences and friends I have come to know, I realize so many people have a variety of situations they encounter, and many people have different ending results depending on where they are. I have looked at the various people I have gotten to know, and many are very positive in their outlook on life overall, although some are more conservative in their approach. Overall, I have noticed a common trend. Those who chose to create a foundation first were the ones who seem the most "stable" in life financially, which usually leads to a more stress-free life overall.

On my radio show on MONEY 1055FM, *Rush Hour For Success*, I often state, "With much money, you have a lot of choices. With a little money, you have little choices. With no money...the choices are chosen for you."

These statements are so true. I have direct experience with the artistic community and also the financial industry which I can say are really a large contrast in the mindset between these two categories.

The mindset between the two categories are extremely different and depending on the choices made, will determine your outcome in life. There is a statement that holds true that if you do the right things, the right things will follow. The question is, "What are the right things?"

I would like to make an analogy of "building a house" to "building a life." If you take the artistic approach, you might try to make the house look incredible with all the aesthetics in place and ensure that the ambience is right. You would then assess what you would need to make the house a reality.

On the other hand, if you were approaching it from a business/financial perspective, you would first see how much you have to work with then build the house according to the budgetary constraints.

While both have its merits, the later would allow you to be more on target knowing what you have to work with in the first place.

## THE RESULTS OF MY CHOICES

As I reflect back on my life, I have been blessed with so many things in this lifetime. Great children, a wonderful wife, a spectacular career, and many friendships that some only dream about. The reality is that I do have some things I wish I would have done differently. I will live with the consequences and rewards of my decisions. My goal is to do whatever I can to maximize my ability to support the greater good. I know that I have many more challenges and barriers ahead that will be sign posts for opportunities to grow or stop. I choose to grow!

## FINALLY!

I am so excited about the stories shared in this book to inspire, motivate, and help us understand just how human we really are. We all face obstacles that will stand in our way. The question is whether those barriers will limit you or be a catalyst for you to do something bigger. Everyone in this book has so many lessons and points of inspiration in their story. In actuality, this book was to be released in 2017...but God knew the timing wasn't quite right. In 2018, we have witnessed so many things that challenge our thinking, divide our country, yet have allowed us to evaluate what is truly important. Individually, we are called to make decisions about our lives and what legacy we will leave behind.

www.ingramcontent.com/pod-product-compliance
Lightning Source LLC
Chambersburg PA
CBHW021224090426
42740CB00006B/365